DEFENDING LIBERTY IN ALABAMA

An Alabama Attorney's Guide for Clients to Effective Criminal Defense

AF808190

Mitchell J. Howie
CRIMINAL DEFENSE ATTORNEY

Copyright © 2023 by Mitchell J. Howie, Esq.

All rights reserved. No part of this publication may be reproduced, distributed, or transmitted in any form or by any means, including photocopying, recording, or other electronic or mechanical methods, without the prior written permission of the publisher, except in the case of brief quotations embodied in critical reviews and certain other noncommercial uses permitted by copyright law. For permission requests, write to the publisher, addressed "Attention: Permissions Coordinator," at the address below.

Jacobs & Whitehall
9600 Escarpment Blvd
Suite 745-282
Austin, TX 78749
(888) 570-7338
www.jacobsandwhitehall.com

Ordering Information:

Quantity sales. Special discounts are available on quantity purchases by corporations, associations, and others. For details, contact the publisher at the address above.

Orders by U.S. trade bookstores and wholesalers. Please contact Jacobs & Whitehall: Tel: (888) 570-7338 or visit www.jacobsandwhitehall.com.

Printed in the United States of America

Published in 2023

ISBN: 978-1-954506-89-3

PREFACE

I wrote this book to help those who are facing the criminal justice system find a lawyer and an advocate who is motivated to assist them and defend their constitutional rights. Far too often I see young and inexperienced alleged criminals end up on the wrong side of the justice system because they simply do not know what they need to know as they determine their course of action and next steps in defending themselves. I write this book with the experience of a practicing attorney for nearly 20 years. In the early stages of my career, I practiced as a prosecutor in the United States Air Force and had another defense attorney tell me that practicing as a defense attorney in the Air Force is like practicing "criminal law without the criminals." While I understand that sentiment, I believe in defending the innocent but also those who are guilty of what they are charged with and are "career criminals" because that is what our justice system requires. I fundamentally believe in 2nd (or 3rd) chances for those facing the criminal justice system and hope this book helps clients find a suitable attorney.

DEDICATION

This book is dedicated to many of my friends I grew up with (in California and Texas) who ended up with permanent criminal records due to not having representation that cared about their future. I truly believe that if some of my friends had legal representation profoundly devoted to zealously representing those that are wrongfully accused, they would not have ended up with criminal records that impacted the entirety of their lives. I hope this book will help individuals facing the criminal justice system find an advocate that is devoted to ensuring a constitutionally adequate and competent criminal defense. Ultimately a client needs a lawyer who will "go to bat" for them against the State in whatever criminal charge they are facing. Hopefully this book can provide some insight to the criminal justice system to those that need it most and when they need it.

ACKNOWLEDGEMENTS

First and foremost, I would like to thank my wife for putting up with all my war stories of my youthful friends who sometimes ended up on the "wrong side of the law." And of course, a big thanks to her for sharing me with my current and future criminal clients. She knows I put my heart and soul into representing all of my clients and sometimes that can lead to a tired husband and father, but she is always there to pick me up and remind me of my priorities. I also want to thank my kids for letting me ask them *voir dire* questions at the dinner table as I remove my legal ease so the jury will understand! Their assistance helps me be the best possible criminal defense attorney. Finally, I want to say thanks to former officer Ryan Manning (who was our last jury trial) for walking his tragic path through the criminal justice system with my firm after being falsely accused of egregious crimes against his child. He had the courage and integrity to trust in the jury system even when I was worried for him about the verdict and I salute him and am proud to call him a friend!

DISCLAIMER

This publication is intended to be used for educational purposes only. No legal advice is being given, and no Attorney-Client relationship is intended to be created by reading this material. The author assumes no liability for any errors or omissions or for how this book or its contents are used or interpreted, or for any consequences resulting directly or indirectly from the use of this book. For legal or any other advice, please consult an experienced Attorney or the appropriate expert, who is aware of the specific facts of your Case and is knowledgeable in the law in your jurisdiction.

Law Office of Mitchell J. Howie

& Associates, P.L.L.C.

102 South Side Square

Huntsville, Alabama 35801

www.mitchellhowie.com

E mail: Info@mitchellhowie.com

Phone: (256) 533-8074

Testimonials

"Let's face it: if you find yourself in the unfortunate position of being charged criminally, your life gets turned upside down until the process is over. Mr. Howie has been my attorney for 2 years now. He's been with me from the very beginning. I can confidently say that he treated my case with the same care and attention that he would give a member of his own family. And when you find yourself having to do battle with the state, trust me- you WANT a legal warrior. Mr. Howie was fantastic about discussing strategy with me and also giving me the pros and cons of each decision. He knows the law inside and out, and he is the best litigator that I've ever seen. I compared it to watching him play chess, while the state played checkers. Some attorneys are just trying to take your money- if that's what you want, more power to you. But if you're like me, and want to fight false allegations, Mr. Howie is the attorney you want. He takes his cases personally, and I am proud to call him a friend after our successful fight against the state. Do yourself a favor and hire an attorney that gives you a legal advantage.

Hire someone that opposing counsel DREADS going up against in court. Hire Mr. Howie."

– Ryan Manning

****

"BEST ATTORNEY IN MADISON COUNTY! Mitchell J. Howie is the best criminal lawyer in Huntsville! He helped me get all the charges against me dismissed and I didn't even have to show up for court! I can't thank Mitchell J. Howie enough for the work he put in to get me the results I needed, he cares about his clients and always responds in a timely and professional manner! If you are looking for a criminal defense attorney in Madison County, look no further and call Huntsville lawyer Mitchell J. Howie today! He is truly the best criminal attorney you can find in Alabama!"

– Julio C. Rodriguez

****

"Best Military Criminal Defense Lawyer in all of Huntsville, Alabama! No one ever expects to need to hire a criminal defense lawyer for themselves, but Mr. Mitchell J. Howie should be your first call if that day comes. My experience working with Mr. Mitchell J. Howie has been

tremendously positive in what was a negative situation. Mr. Howie was honest and straightforward with everything I was encountering and the actions I needed to take. He was always available for any questions I had. He will give you the information you need to make an informed decision. If you are looking for an attorney who treats you like family, you cannot go wrong with Mr. Howie. I highly recommend hiring Mr. Howie for all your Criminal Defense needs."

– *Michael H.*

****

"Best lawyer in town hands down! Probably the best period! I never even made it to court, and charges were dismissed! He was very expedient on getting things figured out from the minute we hired him, all the way down to the day before the court date. He even got work done on his vacation! Madeline, she's the best too! Mr. Howie and Madeline rocked it! I'm one more step closer to seeing my daughter because of these people! Thank you!"

– *Seth B.*

****

Hands down the best criminal defense attorney in the State of Alabama! Mr. Howie will cover every aspect of your case to fight for the best results. I wouldn't waste time speaking with other attorneys, Mitchell Howie will get you the best possible results!

— Jason H.

****

"BEST criminal defense attorney in the Southeast hands down! Highly responsive, professional, and efficient. Mitchell and his team do what they say when they say. Always returns email, texts, and calls. He was very accommodating in my situation and went above and beyond. Don't go to court unprepared. Contact Mitchell Howie, he will definitely have your back and keep the other side honest."

— James A.

****

TABLE OF CONTENTS

ABOUT THE AUTHOR

After passing the bar, I opened my firm in Austin, Texas, initiating my journey into criminal defense. At first, I represented civilians and worked with several criminal defendants, but the military soon beckoned, and I took on the role of a JAG in the United States Air Force which allowed me to prosecute cases across various US Air Force bases. This was my first extensive exposure to criminal law albeit from a prosecutor's perspective.

During my nearly five years of active duty in the military, I was also selected to be a prosecutor for the Department of Justice as a Special Assistant to the US Attorney (SAUSA). In this job, I prosecuted crimes by civilians on military bases (particularly at Pope Air Force Base). Outside of my prosecutor duties in the military, I fulfilled a diverse set of other roles in the military justice system, including assignments as an administrative officer, Article 32 Officer (Preliminary Hearing Officer), and legal advisor to administrative discharge boards.

Although this time on "the other side" gave me invaluable insight and experience, criminal defense was where my heart truly lay. So, after ending my active- duty service in the military in 2009, I reopened my firm in Huntsville, Alabama, with an emphasis on criminal defense.

Since then, I've defended countless criminal defendants in State and Federal Court and have continued to represent service members in military courts martial. I have also assisted service members on the defense side with administrative issues and military justice scenarios to include Article 15s, LORs, and LOCs. As a part of my continued commitment to the legal community and the military justice system, I continue to teach trial advocacy to young JAGs and just helped lead a "TRIALS" course held in Germany August 2023.

In my practice, I have represented thousands of individuals across a spectrum of cases, ranging from low-level traffic violations to severe felony offenses. One of my most significant recent cases involved defending Former Officer Ryan Manning in Jackson County. Due to my client's law enforcement profession and the awful allegations of him causing 15 broken bones to his infant daughter, the case garnered some media attention. Ultimately, the jury acquitted my client, who was obviously extremely satisfied with the case outcome.

Today, my criminal defense practice is based in Alabama, spanning both federal and state jurisdictions. I am still qualified to represent clients in courts martial anywhere in the world, contingent on the specific hiring details and location.

The Benefit Of Having Prosecutorial Insight

Litigation in the Criminal Justice System is inherently adversarial, you constantly face the opposition of the prosecutor and the government trying to refute your arguments and/or present facts contrary to your narrative. Whether this opposition is happening before a judge, or a jury, it is an integral part of the decision-making process in the criminal justice system.

My experience as a prosecutor has given me unique insights. When you're the prosecutor, you shoulder the burden of proof, be it in state, military, or federal criminal jurisdictions. This perspective, of constructing a case with this responsibility, becomes invaluable when you transition to defense.

With this knowledge, a criminal defense attorney can anticipate the prosecutor's approach and try to stay one step ahead while building your defense strategy. It's like having a window into the opponent's playbook, ensuring that you're better equipped to seek the best outcomes for your clients.

Though courtroom dynamics demand an adversarial stance due to conflicting case theories, it doesn't mean animosity should extend beyond professional boundaries. Drawing from my military background, I've always prioritized maintaining collegiality and professionalism with all prosecutors.

Recognizing that they're doing their job—just as I once did—fosters mutual respect. Furthermore, this approach helps in forging constructive relationships with prosecutors. Understanding their position, especially when they lack the discretion to decide a case's direction, cultivates empathy and smoother legal proceedings for my role and, most importantly, for all my firm's criminal defense clients.

What Criminal Defense Means To Me on a Personal Level

Growing up without a father, I found myself in California, closely associated with peers who similarly lacked paternal figures. As often happens in single parent households, some of my acquaintances eventually faced legal troubles during our middle school years. Recognizing that this was a dangerous environment for me to grow up in, my mother made a transformative decision to move us from Richmond, California, to northern Alabama.

This drastic shift was met with great resistance on my part, simply because I resented the sudden change in our lives. Leaving California at 14, I stupidly thought about running away and living with my friend Antoine in one of Richmond's most challenging neighborhoods. As soon as the week after our relocation, I started receiving distressing calls from friends who had been incarcerated due to criminal decisions. Clearly my mother made the right call.

Over the years, witnessing my friends grapple with legal issues and sometimes receiving subpar legal representation deeply affected me. I saw first-hand how proper legal advocacy could have altered their futures, sparing them from criminal records and the enduring consequences that follow. This personal history has fueled my mission to provide robust and effective defense for those who err, whether they've made simple mistakes or have ventured deeper into criminal activities.

Our legal system thrives on effective adversarial representation from both sides. Without a strong criminal defense team on your side, the prosecution can easily overpower inexperienced or passive defense attorneys. I stand firm in my belief and commitment to offering everyone their deserved representation, ensuring justice is not one-sided or *state/government/prosecutor* driven.

The Importance Of Having Support

In my adolescent years, I frequently expressed resentment towards my mother for our move to Huntsville, Alabama. The initial year was especially challenging due to my intense feelings of displacement and anger. However, as time passed and I matured, I found myself repeatedly thanking my mother for her decisive action.

The trajectory of my life shifted because of her determination to provide me with a better environment, far removed from the influences of Richmond. Her sacrifices ensured that I would eventually become a lawyer and a lieutenant colonel in the military. I've often acknowledged her efforts, praising her for not seeking to be my friend but rather a strong parent who made the tough decisions in my best interest.

My Dedication To Helping My Clients Find Second Chances

The reason I am taking the time to explain a bit of my personal biography is because I want anyone taking the time to read this book to recognize that there are advocates that genuinely understand their circumstances and I want them to find an effective attorney no matter what jurisdiction they are facing criminal charges. Drawing from my personal experiences with friends who faced similar adversities, I approach every case without judgment. Every decision, mistake, or path taken by an individual is seen through a lens of understanding.

Whether up against the state of Alabama, the federal government, or the military, I am fiercely dedicated to defending my clients. Each case I undertake resonates deeply, recalling the friends who could not achieve their aspirations due to past mistakes. Every client's narrative serves as a reminder of the stakes involved.

Clients who choose to work with my firm should know that in addition to this sense of empathy, they're gaining a knowledgeable advocate. With a background in both prosecution and defense, I possess a comprehensive understanding of criminal law and the criminal justice system. This dual perspective empowers me to strategize for the most favorable outcomes.

Everyone, at some point, falters or errs. I firmly believe that occasional mistakes shouldn't tarnish one's entire life, hindering their journey towards becoming responsible and productive citizens.

My personal experiences have shown me the harsh reality of missed second chances. In situations where the odds seem insurmountable, my role sometimes shifts to damage control and mitigation. Whether it's seeking diversion, reductions in charges, dismissals, or alternative resolutions, I strive for opportunities that offer my clients a renewed lease on life. The aim is always to ensure that they're not defined solely by a past mistake but are provided an avenue to rebuild and contribute positively to society.

CHAPTER ONE

CASES & CONCERNS

Our firm caters to a wide spectrum of legal situations, emphasizing a nuanced approach that takes the unique circumstances of each client into consideration. Whether defending against severe criminal accusations, or trying to mitigate potential collateral consequences of a criminal conviction our commitment to our clients remains unwavering.

The Concerns Of Criminal Defendants

When criminal defendants approach our firm, their concerns are often universally shared and clear-cut:

1. **Fear of Incarceration:** The overriding anxiety most clients express is their aversion or fear of serving jail time. The prospect of confinement is daunting, and naturally, clients wish to try to avoid it at all costs.
2. **Avoiding Long-Term Probation:** For those who might face an inevitable conviction, an extended probation period is another significant worry. They seek to minimize or eliminate this possibility.
3. **Evading a Permanent Felony Conviction:** A felony conviction can leave an indelible mark on an individual's record, affecting many facets of their life. Clients are sometimes keenly aware of this, and if not, our firm seeks to educate our clients on the permanent stigma of a felony conviction. And as a team we work to sidestep the lasting repercussions of such a felony record.

In essence, clients come to us with the hope of preserving their freedom, ensuring short or no probationary periods, and evading a lifelong stigma from a felony conviction. These concerns guide our defense strategies and inform our counsel in each individual case we take to zealously represent our clients.

A Quick Look Into The Different Types Of Cases We Handle

- **Drug-Related Charges**

We frequently handle cases related to drug possession, distribution or trafficking. Oftentimes, clients are caught in situations where they were merely accompanying a friend involved in such activities. Other times, folks with addiction issues are caught in the criminal justice system. And of course, others may have made a conscious decision to be involved in selling and/or using drugs. No matter the particular circumstance, all of these individuals should expect and receive zealous criminal defense advocacy.

- **Driving Under the Influence (DUI)**

DUI cases are commonplace in every state in the United States. The intricacy of these charges and the defense process surrounding them could fill an entire book. One of the largest impacts these misdemeanor offenses can have on our clients' lives is the charges can take away the client's ability to drive and/or require the client to install expensive monitoring systems in their car which will ensure the client is not drinking before they are able to drive. Our firm has handled hundreds of DUI cases and successfully achieved dismissals, acquittals, and negotiated beneficial plea deals to limit the severe impact of DUI charges on our clients.

- **Sexual Assault Defense**

Sexual crimes like rape, sexual assault, and sex with minors are some of the most severe criminal charges anyone can face. Many if not all of these crimes have mandatory prison sentences and lifetime consequences to include lifetime registration with authorities. If convicted of these sorts of crimes the conviction can even prevent those convicted of "sex crimes" from living in certain areas. Our firm has been notably successful in defending sexual assault cases, which present unique challenges. Clients typically approach us for help on such cases when they've been falsely accused of a sexual assault against a consenting adult. At other times, clients come to us when they are facing (sometimes) false allegations of heinous sex crimes against children. We strive to minimize the lasting effects of sex crimes for all our clients whether the alleged victim is an adult or a child.

- **Burglary and Theft Charges**

Property crimes are another area of the criminal justice system where we represent clients. Sometimes people need help if they are accused of breaking into one's home (Burglary) or stealing from their employer and/or another person. A notable subcategory of theft includes shoplifting incidents at retail giants like Walmart and Target, where individuals can even face criminal allegations for not scanning items correctly at self-checkout counters. Some people, misled by the seeming simplicity of such charges, underestimate their seriousness, leading to theft convictions which can permanently impact the rest of their lives.

- **Homicides**

The most severe crime anyone can be charged with is obviously taking another person's life and the long prison sentences associated with such cases means that clients need zealous representation. While our firm can handle murder cases, we currently do not participate in capital murder trials.

- **Battery, Assault, & Bar Brawls**

Another area of the law involving violent crimes against another person can carry lengthy prison sentences. Physical confrontations, whether spontaneous or premeditated, come under our purview rather frequently and we work to minimize the potential consequences for our clients when they are charged with a crime of violence against another person.

- **Domestic Violence**

A specific offshoot of assault, domestic violence cases are particularly troubling for clients. That is because even a misdemeanor conviction for Domestic Violence triggers additional collateral consequences as detailed in the Lautenberg Amendment which still prohibits gun possession by those convicted of misdemeanor domestic violence. This federal law dictates that any individual convicted of misdemeanor domestic violence is prohibited from bearing firearms. The law's intent remains to get and keep firearms out of the hands of those with domestic violence convictions. This can have profound implications for military personnel and hunters and therefore must be considered when facing domestic violence charges. Therefore, uninformed pleas to reduced charges of domestic violence can still jeopardize careers and/or lifelong passions. Our role involves strategizing to circumvent such inadvertent consequences, either by challenging the allegations to secure a dismissal, or negotiating for non-domestic violence designations of the original alleged charges.

Chapter Two

Navigating Arrest

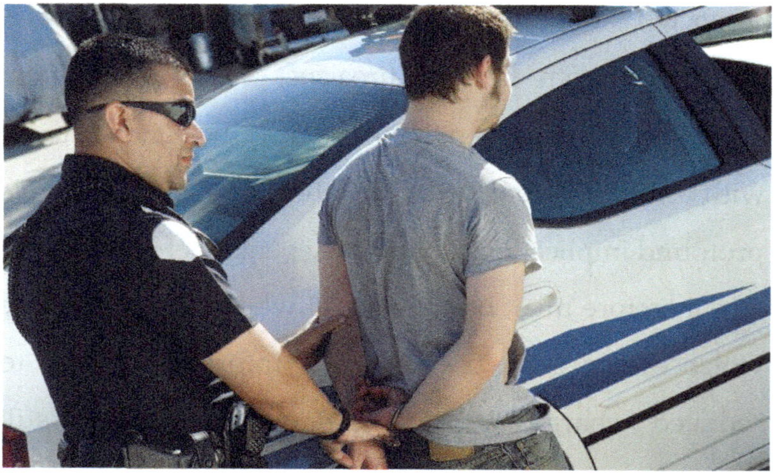

If you've been arrested, or if there's knowledge of an outstanding warrant against you, you are likely stressed out. Here are the pivotal steps you should consider:

1. **Avoid Making Statements:** This is foundational advice in criminal defense. You must refrain from providing any statement to authorities without your attorney present. Often, the case against you might not be fully constructed. By making a

statement, you might inadvertently provide the evidence the State needs for a conviction. Remember, always prioritize your right to remain silent and all other constitutional rights and invoke your right to remain silent when needed.

2. **Invoke Your Right to Counsel:** Should an investigator or police officer question you, be it during an arrest or a routine traffic stop, firmly and clearly assert your right to have legal counsel present. This isn't just about asserting your rights but ensuring they are recognized and trying to ensure you do not waive the right to counsel or other important constitutional rights. Sometimes, failing to explicitly invoke these rights can be seen as waiving them.
3. **Be Cautious, Even with Counsel:** While it's pivotal not to self-incriminate, there are times (seldom as they may be) when, with your attorney's guidance, you may choose to provide a statement. Such instances might arise when there's a genuine misunderstanding that can be clarified. Nonetheless, generally it is always appropriate to

err on the side of caution and stand on your constitutional right to remain silent.

4. **Engage an Attorney Promptly:** If you've already spoken to the authorities, it becomes even more crucial to hire an attorney swiftly. Share all conversations and statements you've had with law enforcement, as this will allow your attorney to craft the most effective criminal defense strategy based on the facts that pertain to your individual circumstances.
5. **Patience is Key:** The criminal justice system can be notoriously slow. Whether navigating the military or civilian system, brace yourself for a drawn-out process. While some cases may see speedy resolutions, the general pace of justice is deliberate and methodical. Understand that this journey will demand patience. As ancient Greek and Chinese philosophers once observed, "the wheels of justice turn slowly but grind exceedingly fine."
6. **Prepare for the Long Haul:** While the temptation might arise to seek a quick resolution, such as accepting a plea deal for a lesser charge, it's

essential to weigh the long-term and sometimes permanent consequences. Quick fixes might come with unforeseen challenges down the line. Instead, equip yourself mentally and emotionally for the upcoming battle, aiming for the most favorable long-term outcome.

7. **Follow your Counsel's Advice:** In all dealings with the legal system, it's best to remain proactive and informed, understanding the gravity of the situation and the potential ramifications of each decision you make. Accordingly, it is imperative that you stay in touch with your attorney and follow all of your counsel's recommendations which typically include ensuring you maintain employment and/or continue your schooling, remain drug free, or seek rehabilitation for your substance abuse problems, and of course, to stay out of further trouble. And stay away from being around those that could lead to more legal problems.

What Happens After Being Arrested

After being arrested, here's a breakdown of the typical sequence of events:

1. **Initial Appearance and Bond Hearing:** Within the first few days following the arrest, you will undergo an initial appearance followed by a bond hearing if you are incarcerated. This is where the court will decide on your eligibility for bail.
2. **Bond Amount:** In most instances in Alabama, you'll be assigned a bond amount. If you're able to pay the stipulated bond amount, you can be immediately released from jail until your court hearing. Bond amounts vary, ranging from as low as $300 for minor misdemeanors to as high as $250,000 to $500,000 to $1,500,000 for serious felony offenses like drug trafficking, sex crimes, and violent felonies.
3. **Unable to Secure Bond:** If you can't afford the bond or if no bond is set for your release, your immediate option is to retain legal representation. Your attorney can then file a motion to set a bond, combined with a demand for a preliminary hearing.

4. **Communications While Incarcerated:** It's paramount to remember that while you are in jail, any conversation you have, both on the phone and with officers, can be used against you in court. And jail calls are always recorded. Remember that officers are not there to assist you in navigating your charges. Always maintain your right to remain silent and refrain from self-incrimination.

The days following an arrest are crucial, and every decision made can significantly impact the trajectory of your case. Safeguarding your rights and obtaining legal representation as soon as possible should always be a priority.

Miranda Rights And The Police

In the civilian criminal context, Miranda Rights become active once a person is in custody. The term "in custody" has spurred much debate and has been subject to various interpretations. Being detained in an interrogation room, especially in handcuffs, is certainly seen as being in custody. While roadside detentions don't necessarily require the reading of Miranda Rights, a client should assume that the constitutional right to remain silent always stands and not answer any questions without the assistance of counsel.

Military individuals, on the other hand, are governed by Article 31 under the Uniform Code of Military Justice (UCMJ), which serves as their right to remain silent and be informed of the suspected offenses BEFORE any questioning begins. Accordingly, if a military member is suspected of wrongdoing, anyone subject to the UCMJ seeking to interrogate them must provide their Article 31 rights before performing any questioning.

Things To Avoid When Facing Arrest

Whether you are a civilian, or military personnel, it's crucial to be cautious about what you divulge. Refrain from granting any permissions for searches, whether it's your residence or vehicle. While there are instances where officers might have valid grounds for a search, they often lean on the individual's consent. To avoid unintentionally providing evidence against yourself, always assert your rights, and remember that you're not obliged to permit searches without a warrant.

Who To Contact Once Arrested

Upon arrest, you're usually allowed a phone call. It's recommended to contact someone who can help with your bail since attorneys are generally ethically restricted from posting your bond. After securing your release, immediately get in touch with your attorney. Several legal deadlines are crucial, such as the 10-day period for contesting a DUI license suspension or the month-long window to demand a preliminary hearing for felony cases in Alabama. Failing to adhere to these timelines can lead to forfeiting your rights.

Bond Eligibility

In Alabama, the law previously stipulated that all non-capital cases and even some capital cases qualified for bail and bond. However, with the recent passage of "Aniah's Law" in 2022 (which was an amendment to the Alabama Constitution) the law in Alabama was changed and now Alabama Judges can use the law to deny bond to "violent offenders." The practical application of setting a bond and the issuance of a bond can vary from county to county throughout Alabama. For example, if an investigator deems you a genuine threat to society, they might set an exorbitantly high bond in the hopes that you do not hire an attorney to challenge the bond or with the expectation that the judge will refuse to reduce the amount because the judge may agree with the investigator. In such scenarios, it's imperative to hire an attorney who can attempt to reduce the bond amount, ensuring you're not stuck in jail while awaiting your court dates and planning your defense.

CHAPTER THREE

PREPARING FOR COURT

Steps To Take After Being Released From Jail

Upon release from jail, if you haven't yet retained an attorney, it's essential to do so promptly. While you will have an initial appearance scheduled in Madison County's District Court to discuss the charges against you and have counsel appointed if you cannot afford representation, having legal representation prior to this date, will help ensure you are well-prepared for your criminal defense. Crucially, for felony charges there's only a 30 day window to demand a preliminary hearing. Thus, an early appointment with an attorney facilitates swift action on your case.

If your case is within Alabama, the details can typically be accessed through the Alabama E filing system (Alacourt), covering all counties in the state. In situations where the state has brought charges against you, early legal consultation is pivotal for building a robust and effective criminal defense.

One common pitfall post-release is neglecting to follow the conditions of your bond. Complying with these conditions, which often stipulate where you can and cannot go, or what activities you must avoid, is vital. Failing to adhere to your bond requirements could lead to bond revocation, meaning you might find yourself back in jail, either awaiting another bond hearing and/or remaining there until trial.

A crucial note for DUI cases: there's a 10-day window to request an administrative hearing with the state to review the suspension of your license in civil court. Failing to act within this timeframe results in a waiver of this right. To navigate this process effectively, attorney intervention is almost always necessary.

Things To Avoid After Being Released From Jail

Post-release, it's of paramount importance to steer clear of any further legal troubles. Avoid situations or individuals that might embroil you in further legal complications, as any additional infractions could lead to the revocation of your bond and subsequent return to jail.

Maintain a discreet profile, especially when discussing your case. This is consistent with the advice before arrest: do not discuss your case with anyone apart from your legal counsel. Remember, conversations, especially those made using jail phones, are always recorded. Such recordings have, in numerous instances both in Madison County and nationally, proven incriminating. Always prioritize discretion to avoid jeopardizing your defense.

Advantages Of Seeking An Attorney Early

Securing an attorney at the outset can offer various strategic advantages. For instance, there might be a chance to meet with the case's investigator or prosecutor, possibly resolving the matter without official charges. This is particularly relevant in cases of misunderstandings or when evidence exists that can easily exonerate the accused, such as strong and undisputed alibi evidence.

However, it's far more common for the state to have already carried out a detailed investigation, with its factual understanding differing from that of the accused. In such scenarios, engaging a defense attorney early helps to ensure that you can counteract the state's case effectively. The defense attorney will be equipped to engage necessary experts, mirroring the state's preparations. Engaging legal counsel both pre-arrest or post-arrest is crucial, especially to safeguard rights like preliminary hearings in District Court for felony cases in Alabama and to properly prepare for trial.

There can be instances where individuals face direct indictments (thereby sending the Defendant directly to Circuit Court in Alabama), bypassing their right to preliminary hearings. When this happens, the state may be prepared with its experts and a delayed defense can put the accused at a distinct disadvantage, especially concerning timelines for securing and preparing expert witnesses.

Critical Information To Give Your Attorney

When consulting your attorney, transparency is crucial. Firstly, and probably most importantly, you must lay out the facts surrounding the charges and your criminal record. Always prioritize honesty; misleading your attorney can jeopardize your defense. Once the attorney is apprised of the facts, they are ethically bound to them. This means if, during a trial, a client wishes to testify in a manner inconsistent with the initial facts shared, the attorney faces ethical challenges that could require withdrawal by the criminal defense attorney. Clients must understand that their attorney will work based on the facts provided, making truthfulness vital.

Next, your legal history plays a pivotal role. This includes disclosing even minor infractions like speeding tickets and extends to misdemeanors and felonies, regardless of conviction status. Any past charges, even if they didn't result in convictions, are vital. Withholding such details could lead the attorney down an unproductive strategic path, which might be incompatible with your complete legal history.

In short: The more your attorney knows, the better they can tailor a defense strategy for your unique circumstances.

The Importance Of Transparency

All individuals, including attorneys, value trust and honesty. Clients should recognize the significance of maintaining a forthright relationship with their legal counsel. When clients conceal information or provide misleading details, they metaphorically push their attorney out on a fragile branch. For instance, an attorney may end up presenting specific facts to a prosecutor during a negotiation, based on the client's input. And the prosecutor may be able to easily refute the client's factual representations, particularly concerning the Defendant's past criminal history. If your attorney discovers contradictions in the input from the client and from the prosecutor, it fundamentally jeopardizes the defense.

Consider a scenario where a prosecutor contradicts the attorney's understanding of a case, citing prior misdemeanors the client failed to disclose. Such situations can tarnish the credibility of both the client and their defense strategy. While the attorney's reputation might recover, the prosecution will likely become wary of any future negotiations with the individual defendant, especially if they believe the client has deceived their own lawyer.

Misleading one's attorney can have repercussions throughout the immediate case. Prosecutors might be less inclined to consider alternative solutions or plea bargains, given their doubts about the client's honesty. This could negatively affect case outcomes and overall defense strategies.

Therefore, transparency is paramount. Trust is foundational to any relationship, be it personal or professional. Without it, effective communication and mutual understanding become challenging, if not impossible. Just as one would expect openness in relationships with spouses and/or partners, the attorney-client bond also thrives on mutual trust and respect.

Court Appearances And Attendance

When navigating the legal system, your presence in court is generally expected and required unless advised otherwise by your attorney. Let's break this down using the context of criminal cases in Alabama:

1. **Initial Appearance:** If you're charged with a felony and have secured bail, you'll be scheduled for an initial appearance in district court. This appearance is primarily to clarify the charges against you and to assign legal representation if you can't afford legal representation.

   However, if you intend to hire an attorney before this, the need for the initial appearance might be moot. For instance, if my firm is retained before this date, we file various motions, such as a notice of appearance, a motion for a speedy trial, and other pre-trial motions, all to safeguard the client's rights. This can render the initial appearance unnecessary, moving the first court date to the preliminary hearing stage.

2. **Preliminary Hearing:** This serves as a probable cause hearing prior to an indictment and allows the Defendant and their team to get a preview of the evidence the State is relying on to bring the charges. While certain case law in Alabama explains that a defendant's presence isn't mandatory, I always advise my clients to attend if at all possible. This hearing determines if there's probable cause to believe you committed the crime and if the case will move forward.

   To put this into perspective, achieving 'probable cause' is a minimal hurdle for prosecutors, whereas 'Beyond A Reasonable Doubt' is significantly higher. Preliminary hearings can sometimes provide valuable evidence that would not be accessible through regular "paper discovery." However, sometimes it's tactically beneficial to waive this hearing to access police reports and other paperwork. The particular strategy for your case will need to be discussed with your counsel and depends on the facts and the law applicable to your individual case.

3. **Indictments:** After the preliminary hearing, your next court appearance would generally be post-indictment. Indictments in Madison County, Alabama, might issue generally anywhere from a year to two years post the alleged incident. During this interval, as our firm's client, we will be diligently gathering facts, identifying witnesses, and coordinating with private investigators and experts. The indictment process involves a grand jury and is confidential, meaning you are not going to be part of the grand jury proceedings.
4. **Subsequent Proceedings:** Following the indictment, you'll have multiple dates in circuit court, including arraignments, various pre-trial dates and the actual trial. Some judges may also schedule *status calls* to ensure a smooth process. In Madison County's Circuit Court, there might be three or more dates leading up to the trial. While you might not be

required to attend all appearances, it's crucial to consult with your attorney and to assume you must be present for all court appearances unless and until instructed otherwise by your attorney. Ultimately and obviously, you'll definitely need to be present for the criminal jury trial.

Remember, while this outlines a typical court attendance process, each case is unique. Variables like individual county practices and case backlog can cause delays, meaning you'll likely attend court multiple times before your case concludes.

How To Assist Your Attorney In Your Case

Achieving the best possible outcome in your case requires diligent cooperation with your counsel. Always maintain open lines of communication with both your attorney and any private investigator hired by you or your firm. This constant interaction ensures that you're aligned with your legal team's strategy and approach.

Furthermore, it's vital to remain cautious and avoid any situation that might jeopardize your case. If you're connected with your accusers (or their friends) on platforms like Facebook or Twitter (X), it's crucial to monitor their activity. Informative or contradictory posts they share can be relayed to your attorney and private investigators for potential use in your defense. Equally important is for you to not post anything on social media accounts that could be used against you.

How Your Record Affects Your Case

The impact of your past record on your current case can be multifaceted. Your attorney will meticulously assess past arrests, convictions, and the specifics of your present charge. They will consider:

- The elapsed time since previous incidents.
- Whether past offenses were for violent crimes.
- Any cases where a past charge might have been unwarranted.

Possessing a criminal history could signal to the prosecution your familiarity with the legal system. For example, if you're facing your eighth felony charge and have served prison time before, it may disqualify you for certain lenient treatments, such as diversion programs. Notably, the first felony is pivotal, as it marks you as a felon and may reduce future opportunities.

However, there's a silver lining. If your record is clean, your attorney can frame your situation as a *one-off mistake or growing pains*, striving for a resolution that recognizes this.

In some states, like Alabama, local laws, such as the Habitual Felony Offender Act, can have significant implications. Such legislation can sway the outcome based on your history. If your past is tainted with multiple felonies, it's imperative your attorney knows. With all information at hand, they can:

- Develop a strategy to achieve a probation sentence.
- Aim to curtail any jail time.
- Look into alternatives, like the Supervised Electronic Detention Program (SEDP), which is akin to house arrest in specific areas like Madison County, or Community Corrections Program (CCP) or Active Work Release (AWR).

CHAPTER FOUR

MORE COMPLEX CASES

The Complexity Of DUI, Sex Crime Cases and Child Abuse Cases

DUI cases present unique challenges, particularly concerning the immediate suspension of one's driver's license. You'll need:

- An attorney proficient in preserving your driving privileges, especially if your job relies on it.
- Legal expertise in navigating scientific issues such as breath tests, blood tests, refusals, and dealing

with high breath test results. There are specialized experts who can assist in these matters.

Sex crime cases, especially those involving minors, demand a distinct level of expertise. Recent years have led to an increase in these sorts of cases which has led to my firm working extensively on such cases. Our experience in these cases has highlighted the importance of securing an attorney who is:

- Knowledgeable about delayed reporting scenarios.
- Able to utilize memory experts, highlighting the potential inaccuracies of memory.
- Able to utilize and combat the pseudo "scientific evidence" the State relies on in these cases.

Moreover, the term "forensic interview" refers to the procedures undertaken with children in these situations. There's a growing infrastructure dedicated to addressing child sexual assault, reminiscent of the large-scale systems President Eisenhower once cautioned against in the context of the military. While the primary goal of child protection is inherently a noble and just goal, one must remember:

- Children, like adults, can make mistakes, misremember, or even lie.
- Children are particularly susceptible to manipulation and suggestibility.
- There's a risk of premature judgment in our quest to protect children. This haste can result in family separations, damaged marriages, and even the unjust imprisonment of innocent individuals.

Choosing an attorney well-versed in the scientific aspects of these cases and connected with expert witnesses is crucial. To highlight this, one might consider a case that our firm recently handled in Jackson County, Alabama, involving child abuse allegations against former police officer Ryan Manning. Mr. Manning was accused of inflicting numerous fractures on his eight-week-old child, the immediate assumption by medical professionals and the legal system was intentional abuse by the Father. Even though both parents initially were potential suspects upon arriving at the hospital with their injured child.

Nearly two years later, the case ended in acquittal after a week-long trial, however, the damage already done was extensive. The medical system's assumptions and the state's initial pressure led to familial separation while the State pressured the mother to "point the finger" at the Father (which caused all parents to be distanced from the child). The erroneous and absurd medical assumption of "abuse until proven otherwise" led to the State seeking to "find the bad guy" instead of seeking reasonable and alternative explanations of innocence.

Sadly, the state even overlooked an early expert opinion pointing to a potential vitamin D deficiency resulting in brittle bones of the child. In their haste, the state's actions led to a family's devastation, to include the divorce of the parents, thereby depriving a child of a two-parent household during her formative years. Clearly the rush to judgment resulted in consequences that were both tragic and irrevocable.

The Necessity of an Expert Attorney in Complex Cases

Having an attorney who is skilled in identifying potential pitfalls and prepared to acknowledge the limits of their scientific knowledge is critical, particularly when dealing with intricate cases like child abuse or sex crimes.

In situations where the state is zealously dedicated to "protecting children", they might, at times, proceed in ways that can be deemed misguided or even inappropriate, especially when allegations are baseless.

For instance, in the case mentioned above, our defense enlisted two expert witnesses. The first, an orthopedic surgeon, explained early on that this was not a clear-cut case of intentional abuse. The second expert assessed the x-rays, analyzed the Mother's deficiency in Vitamin D at the time of the birth, and corroborated the father's version of events (in that he had involuntarily clenched the child close to his chest when he dozed off) was a reasonable explanation of innocence.

This very plausible non-abusive explanation was, unfortunately, overlooked by the state. Without diligent and informed representation, there is no telling what kind of outcome our client may have faced as a result. As such, working with an attorney who is familiar with such intricacies should be non-negotiable for clients.

Furthermore, in cases related to sex crimes the implications are profound (especially when minors are involved). Convictions of these crimes lead to mandatory registration as a lifetime sex offender under the Sexual Offender Registration Notification Act (SORNA). This registration entails:

- Strict limitations on living proximities to schools and/or "childcare facilities."
- Ever-expanding restrictions that often force individuals to reside in isolated areas.
- Regular mandatory reporting, impacting daily life indefinitely.

Given the gravity of these consequences, securing an attorney cognizant of these intricacies is of paramount importance.

Representing Military Personnel In Court

Having extensive experience in military courts martial, notably from my time as a prosecutor in the military, has allowed me to gain insights that are often missed by many civilian criminal defense attorneys. In nearly 5 years of serving the country on active duty, I was frequently involved in jury trials, something that is more common in military settings (at least for young lawyers) than on the civilian criminal defense side. This wealth of experience, paired with my current service as a lieutenant colonel in the reserves, grants me a unique understanding of military legal challenges.

For military personnel, the stakes of a criminal charge are particularly high:

- **Professional Responsibilities and Restrictions:** The obligations and limitations inherent to military life far surpass those of civilian professions. A civilian arrest or conviction might not always influence someone's standing at a civilian job, but in the military, even an arrest can have severe impacts due to the revered uniform worn.
- **Career Implications:** Any "on-duty or off-duty" incidents involving military personnel can jeopardize their career, sometimes even ending it. Military policy favors exercising jurisdiction over its members. This means that legal troubles outside

the confines of the military could translate to facing a court-martial rather than a civilian criminal court.

- **In-depth Understanding Required:** To navigate such complex scenarios, you require an attorney well-versed in the military's internal workings. The repercussions for military personnel, even for seemingly minor charges, can be severe.

  For instance, even a misdemeanor domestic violence charge triggering the Lautenberg Amendment's prohibition could be a career-ending event. As such, it's crucial for your legal representation to be deeply familiar with the obligations unique to military service to help ensure any negative impacts on your career are minimized or completely negated.

- **Liaison with Military Leadership:** Ideally, you should opt for legal representation willing to engage with your military superiors, like your commander or first sergeant. A proactive approach to communicating your side of the story can often lead to garnering support from the command structure, which can be invaluable during your criminal proceedings.

In short: Military personnel facing legal challenges need specialized legal support that can only be offered by those who truly understand the nuances of military life and service and the interconnection between the current criminal charges and their potential impact upon the client's military service.

CHAPTER FIVE

SETTLING AND SENTENCING

Deciding Between Plea Offers and Going to Trial to Seek Full Dismissal

The decision between accepting a plea offer or going to trial to pursue a full acquittal largely rests on the client's personal and professional circumstances:

- **Client Goals:** The foundation of any decision lies in the client's objectives. For instance, those holding a top-secret security clearance, or some other high level job (that they can maintain while facing criminal charges) will likely need a full acquittal and dismissal of all charges. The nature of the charge and the client's situation often dictate the best path forward.

- **Legal Analysis:** After understanding the client's needs, it's essential to weigh the charges against the provable facts. Accepting a plea is usually advised if the client is genuinely guilty or if there's a significant likelihood of conviction during a trial. Every trial is unpredictable due to varying juror perspectives, making it critical to consider all facets before making a decision.

Plea Offers for First-Time Offenders

First-time offenders face unique challenges and considerations:

- **Felony Implications:** A first felony charge and conviction can have lasting consequences. Even if sentencing guidelines suggest no jail time, accepting a felony plea is typically not advisable, especially for first-time offenders. At our firm we often advise clients "the first felony is the worst felony" due to the lifelong collateral consequences.

- **Violent Crimes:** In cases of violent crimes, prosecutors may initially propose a plea deal with no jail time, thereby "only" seeking a felony conviction. Thorough analysis is needed to decide whether to accept such an offer.
- **Diversion Programs:** These are alternatives to traditional sentencing. Offenders admit guilt and undergo a program akin to probation. Successful completion results in the full dismissal of charges.

Repeat Offenders

Subsequent offenses come with heightened stakes:

- **Guidelines Offense:** While first and second-time offenders might receive probation sentences under the guidelines, repeated offenses increase the likelihood of incarceration.
- **Multiple Offenses:** Habitual offenders, especially by the third, fourth, or fifth offense, risk harsher penalties. Non-violent or non-sex crimes might still be subject to sentencing guidelines, however,

even those guidelines can dictate prison time for repeat offenders.

- **Alternatives to Prison:** In circumstances where prison is recommended, other alternatives might be explored, such as electronic monitoring, work release, or community corrections, to minimize jail time.

Every situation demands a tailored approach. Understanding the client's needs, the nature of the crime, and the potential consequences are crucial for determining the most advantageous course of action.

Out-of-Court Settlements

Most cases, whether civil or criminal, are typically settled out of court without necessitating a jury trial. Resolutions can vary, including:

- Full dismissal of charges.
- Payment of court costs leading to full dismissal.
- Reduction of the original charge to a misdemeanor or a less severe felony.

- Re-designating a Domestic Violence crime to another classification to avoid the Lautenberg Amendment prohibition of possessing firearms.
- Re-designating a sex crime to another classification to avoid mandatory registration under the Sexual Offender Registration Notification Act (SORNA).

Case Dismissal: Implications for Charges and Records

The effect of a dismissal on your record is contingent on the dismissal type:

- **Full Dismissal:** If the state acknowledges they targeted the wrong person and dismisses the case, it's crucial to request a dismissal "with prejudice." Subsequently, one might be eligible for expungement as soon as possible and thereby "erase" the arrest from one's record as if it never occurred.
- **Reduced Charge:** If the charge is downgraded (e.g., from a felony assault to a misdemeanor assault) and a plea deal is accepted, the offender must adhere to the plea deal's terms and conditions. For instance, if the deal includes probation with a suspended

sentence (i.e. potential six-month jail term hanging over the offender's head while the Defendant completes probation) then the Defendant's failure to adhere to the probation terms might result in the Defendant serving the suspended jail sentence (or a portion thereof).

- **Dismissal Does Not Remove the Arrest Record:** Sometimes, charges are dismissed, leaving only an arrest on the client's record. This arrest can sometimes be expunged, ensuring it does not remain on the client's record, but other times it may not be eligible for expungement.
- **Conviction Records:** Convictions, even misdemeanor convictions, can follow you for the rest of your life. You cannot expect to have convictions removed except through pardons which are lengthy, expensive and unlikely.

Conviction And Sentencing

If you're convicted of a charge after a trial by a jury, you may qualify for an appeal bond and a subsequent sentencing hearing. Typically, the court schedules a sentencing hearing a few months post-trial. In State Criminal Courts in Alabama, after receiving the pre-sentence investigation report, the judge determines your sentence.

In contrast, the military justice system proceeds differently. At Courts Martial, sentencing occurs immediately following a conviction which is unlike Alabama, where several months might pass before the sentencing date. When determining your sentence, the judge will consider:

- Your background.
- Whether the offense is governed by sentencing guidelines.
- The impact on the victim.
- If you've accepted responsibility for the crime.
- The nature of the crime (whether violent or not).
- Your reputation within the community.
- Recommendations from community members.
- Feedback from the victim and the victim's family, especially for violent crimes.

However, one of the main aspects that govern your sentence is the classification of the crime for which you were convicted. The lawful punishments for the various crimes in Alabama are as follows:

Misdemeanor Offenses

- **Class C Misdemeanor:** Potential sentencing of up to 3 months in jail and a fine up to $500.
- **Class B Misdemeanor:** Potential sentencing of up to 6 months in jail and a fine up to $3,000.
- **Class A Misdemeanor:** Potential sentencing of up to 365 days in jail and a fine up to $6,000.

Felony Offenses

- **Class D felony:** Not less than 1 year and 1 day, and not more than 5 years in the state penitentiary and a fine not to exceed $7,500.
- **Class C felony:** Not less than 1 year and 1 day and not more than 10 years imprisonment in the state penitentiary and a fine not to exceed $15,000.

- **Class B felony:** Not less than 2 years and not more than 20 years imprisonment in the state penitentiary and a fine not to exceed $30,000.
- **Class A felony:** Not less than 10 years and not more than life, or 99 years imprisonment in the state penitentiary and a fine not to exceed $60,000.

This classification, combined with the specific facts of the charges against you, provides the initial framework for sentencing. Only after considering these foundational elements does the judge weigh the other aforementioned factors.

Improving Your Chances Before Sentencing

To enhance the likelihood of a more lenient sentence, consider the following actions:

- Procure letters of recommendation.
- Present character witnesses in court.
- Maintain consistent employment or be actively involved in furthering your education.
- Exhibit drug-free behavior and ensure you can pass a drug test.

- Gather recommendations from employers, friends, or respected community members.
- Abstain from any illegal activities.

By diligently following these steps, you position yourself favorably, enabling your attorney to persuasively argue for leniency or mercy during your sentencing.

The Process Of Probation

When it comes to dealing with your probation officer, adherence to all rules and punctuality in your meetings and calls are paramount. The following are guidelines to ensure you maintain a positive relationship with your probation officer:

- Always act promptly and respectfully. If asked to jump, metaphorically speaking, do so promptly.
- Promptly and Consistently pay all fines and fees.
- Arrive for appointments on time, ideally 10 minutes early.
- Demonstrating punctuality and compliance can expedite the end of your probation period.

If you exhibit any lapses, such as failing to attend meetings, your probation officer may have grounds to seek revocation of the probationary period. Such a revocation could lead to you serving the entirety of your sentence. For instance, as a first-time offender with a reduced charge (from a violent to nonviolent offense), the prosecutor might sentence you to a maximum of 10 years for a class C felony but place you on a two-year probation. Abiding by your probation terms effectively becomes your way to avoid 10 years of incarceration.

However, there's an essential distinction to note: while probation officers might stress the importance of covering fees and fines, if you genuinely lack the financial means, you cannot legally be incarcerated solely for your inability to pay. But neglecting to attend probation meetings, or court appearances, is a valid ground for jail time to be imposed. Accordingly, even if you can't pay, your presence is mandatory. If faced with such challenges, seek legal advice. As an attorney, I often counsel clients to ensure that financial hardships don't jeopardize their probation status.

Strict adherence to probation terms is non-negotiable. If, for example, you have a 10-year sentence as a suspended sentence, any lapses—like missing appointments or incurring new charges—can trigger a revocation request from your probation officer. The standard for probation revocation is not as stringent as courtroom convictions. A judge simply needs to be "reasonably satisfied" that your probation terms have been breached or that a new offense was committed. Such breaches can, in many cases, lead to the imposition of the entirety of the suspended sentence. Accordingly, it is imperative to always comply with your probation terms and conditions.

Alternative Sentences To Jail Time

Navigating the legal landscape, several alternatives to traditional jail time emerge, each offering unique opportunities for those looking to avoid incarceration. Some typical alternative dispositions and alternative sentences are as follows:

Community Service

This approach can serve dual purposes. In certain scenarios, one can achieve a complete dismissal of charges through their community service without entering into a formal diversion program. Similarly, it might be integrated into formal diversion programs. Here, an admission of guilt may be necessary, and once a predetermined number of community service hours are completed, the charges can be dismissed.

Drug Court

A distinct legal avenue available to those who have a drug problem, the Drug Court requires an initial plea. Its primary aim is to offer essential services to ensure individuals don't revert to drug use. Completion of the program results in the dismissal of charges. Conversely, failing the course typically subjects the individual to incarceration and conviction of the initial charges associated with their plea.

Mental Health Court

Tailored to address underlying mental health issues for Defendants, this court often prescribes counseling and, when necessary, medication. Like the Drug Court, entry to this court demands an initial plea. Successfully navigating the program leads to a dismissal of charges, while failure confronts participants to incarceration and conviction of the initial charges associated with their plea.

Diversion Programs

Distinct from specific pleas, these programs hinge on an admission of guilt. The experience can vary based on the locality but often mirrors a probationary framework prior to any conviction. Participants voluntarily undertake specific tasks, reporting when necessary and paying all necessary costs. Achieving all requirements results in the dismissal of charges.

Veterans Court

These courts are created specifically to assist Military Veterans. Typically, Veteran's Court Programs mandate an initial plea to the underlying charge. The services provided are specialized for veterans, addressing concerns like drug and alcohol addiction, PTSD, and other psychiatric conditions. Meeting all the program's terms leads to a graduation and dismissal of all charges.

In summary, these alternative pathways can significantly influence one's legal journey, offering reprieves from traditional sentences. However, their success hinges on rigorous adherence to each program's conditions and requirements.

CHAPTER SIX

THE ROLE OF AN ATTORNEY

The Importance Of Legal Representation

Choosing to navigate your case without the guidance of an attorney can lead to undesired and irrevocable outcomes. A common adage in the legal realm posits, "If you represent yourself, you have a fool for a client." This saying holds true for both legal professionals and laypeople venturing into representing themselves in civil and/or criminal proceedings.

When you decide to represent yourself:

- You lack insight into the legal intricacies surrounding your case.
- You may be unaware of standard practices related to situations like yours.
- Your ability to argue for leniency may be significantly compromised compared to someone well-versed in law.

Historical observations reveal disparities in negotiation outcomes between prosecutors and defense attorneys versus self-represented individuals. The terms negotiated by a defense attorney often differ vastly in scope and quality from those negotiated by those without legal counsel. Thus, self-representation, especially in criminal matters, can be perilous.

There's much at stake when facing criminal charges, including the potential for enduring and permanent ramifications, particularly with felonies. Understanding the implications is crucial. An adept criminal defense attorney not only clarifies these potential consequences but can also devise strategies to reduce, manage, or evade them entirely.

Therefore, even if you're inclined to plead guilty, securing legal representation is imperative. It ensures that you will have an advocate who will fight to obtain the most favorable outcome and equips you with a comprehensive understanding of any subsequent ramifications related to a guilty plea or verdict.

Criteria for Selecting an Attorney

When hiring legal representation, it's paramount to make an informed decision. Here's a guideline on what to prioritize and what red flags to be cautious of:

Essential Qualities:

1. **Experience in Trials:** It's crucial to engage someone who has a proven track record in handling cases and has actively participated in bench and jury trials.
2. **Expertise in Criminal Defense:** Seek an attorney who has dedicated many years of researching and practicing criminal defense.

3. **Background as a Prosecutor:** An attorney with experience as a former prosecutor brings a unique perspective, having been on both sides of our adversarial criminal justice system. This dual perspective can be leveraged to benefit your case.
4. **Rapport and Trustworthiness:** It's essential to feel that your attorney genuinely has your best interests at heart.
5. **Understanding of Collateral Consequences:** A knowledgeable attorney comprehends the long-term implications of a criminal conviction and prioritizes addressing these concerns.

Red Flags to Avoid:

1. **Lack of Trial Experience:** Be cautious of attorneys who haven't participated in any jury trials.
2. **Rushing Towards a Plea:** If an attorney insists on accepting the first plea offer without careful consideration, it might indicate a lack of commitment to fully explore all options. Though in rare instances, there might be time-sensitive plea offers, an experienced defense lawyer can usually navigate such situations for the client's benefit.

3. **Inadequate Criminal Defense Skills:** It's a concern if the attorney lacks expertise specifically in criminal defense.
4. **Neglecting Collateral Consequences:** If the attorney doesn't emphasize the long-term ramifications of a conviction, especially a felony, it might indicate a lack of comprehensive understanding of all facets of the criminal justice system.

To conclude, when in the process of hiring legal representation, remember that it's essential to prioritize experience, expertise, and trustworthiness. Always be vigilant of any red flags that may arise during your consultations and research.

What Our Firm Offers You

Choosing our firm ensures that you are selecting a partner who is wholly committed to securing the most favorable outcome for your unique situation. Here's a snapshot of what you can expect:

1. **Dedication:** Our foremost commitment is to guide you towards the best possible resolution tailored to your needs.
2. **Understanding Your Goals:** We don't just focus on the current case. We want to understand your long-term aspirations, whether they relate to your career, personal growth, or future life choices. This holistic approach helps us consider every possible ramification of the current case on your future.
3. **Customized Analysis:** By understanding your background and future goals, combined with an expert interpretation of the law, we craft strategies that align with your personal circumstances and desired outcome.
4. **Transparency:** When we represent you, expect complete clarity and transparent advice. We will elucidate the potential consequences of a conviction in your specific charge and explore possible alternatives that could reduce the severity of your case. Attempting to navigate the legal waters on your own can be treacherous; our expertise can be your compass.

5. **Preparedness for Trial:** In situations where alternative resolutions might not be viable due to the gravity of charges or the stance of the prosecution, rest assured that our team is primed to defend you zealously at any necessary jury trial. We bring extensive experience, having fought and won simple drug cases, assaults, burglaries, thefts, DUIs, Domestic Violence, to complex cases like, drug trafficking, sex crimes, and horrific child abuse crimes.
6. **Track Record of Success:** Our recent jury trials in Alabama have resulted in "not guilty" verdicts. While every case is unique and past successes certainly do NOT guarantee future outcomes, our commitment to fighting for our clients never wavers.
7. **Protecting the Innocent:** Representing an innocent client is a weighty responsibility—one we take extremely seriously. Our goal is not just to win, but to ensure justice prevails.
8. **Guided Decision Making:** While we offer expert counsel, we always remember that the ultimate

decision rests with you. Whether you opt for a jury trial, or to consider and accept plea bargains or other alternatives offered, our role is to present you with all the options and possible outcomes and fight for the best possible outcome.

Our firm isn't just about legal representation—it's about partnership, understanding, and relentless pursuit of justice. When you choose us, you're not just getting a lawyer; you're gaining an advocate dedicated to your cause. As part of our commitment to educate, we are including a felony information pamphlet that we provide to all of our felony clients to explain the "nuts and the bolts" of the felony process in the State of Alabama. You can find it on the next pages in this chapter. Additionally, in the appendix we are including all the plea forms (not because we want people to plead guilty) but to help educate the general public on the constitutional rights discussed at every plea and sentence lengths for different types of charges.

FELONY INFORMATION PAMPHLET

NAME: *"UNLUCKY CLIENT #1001"*

CASE NO. "DC 23-1234 & 1235-MADISON COUNTY"

RANGE OF PUNISHMENT-GUIDELINES OFFENSE

Along with this pamphlet I have been provided and acknowledge receipt of the guidelines worksheets in determining the range of punishment I am facing if convicted.

RANGE OF PUNISHMENT IF NOT A GUIDELINES OFFENSE

CHARGE	CLASS	NLT	NMT	FINE UP TO
	A Felony	10 years	99 years or Life	$ 60,000.00
	B Felony	2 years	20 years	$ 30,000.00
	C Felony	1 year + 1 day	10 years	$ 15,000.00
	D Felony	1 year + 1 day	5 years	$7,500.00

If you have previous felony convictions, we will go over the enhanced or enlarged sentencing range pursuant to the Habitual Felony Offender Sentencing Act in the discussion of your trial rights.

If you are convicted by trial or by guilty plea, you will be sentenced to a term of confinement within the above range of punishments. You **may** be eligible for probation or other sentence diversions upon application to the court. The court **will** also order that you pay **court costs**, the **fees of your court appointed attorney**, **restitution to the victim** in the case, a **Victim Compensation Assessment** to the Alabama Crime Victims Compensation Commission in Montgomery of not less than $50.00 and not more than $10,000.00. Upon conviction of any felony offense, or a violent offense, you will also be ordered to submit a saliva sample for **DNA** typing. You will also be ordered to pay a **$2.00 DNA database fee**.

The law requires that you make arrangements to pay all the court ordered money through the court within a prearranged period of time. In the event no arrangement is made or if the money is not paid as arranged, the District Attorney's Office will undertake to collect the total amount due plus an additional **30% collection fee**. (Act 94-413; Section 12-17-225.4, Code of Alabama of 1975)

In the event that you are convicted by guilty plea or by trial to any offense and are sentenced to confinement to the Madison County Jail, the judge can order that you pay **over $48.00 per day as housing and maintenance associated with your incarceration plus actual medical expenses** incurred on your behalf. Those sums will be taxed to you as court costs. (Section 14-6-22, Code of Alabama of 1975)

Collateral Consequences Of A Conviction Of A Criminal Offense

In the event that you are convicted of a criminal offense, there may be collateral or civil penalties that you may face in addition to the punishments outlined above. Conviction of a criminal offense may result in the loss of the following:

Right to Vote	Right to Hold Public Office
Right to Serve on a Jury	Right to Possess a Firearm
Right to be a Licensed Professional	Social Security benefits
Eligibility to Adopt a Child	Right to Become a Foster Parent

Eligibility for Public Housing Driving Privileges

Eligibility for Food Stamps Eligibility for other Public Assistance

Educational Loans

Upon your release from probation, parole or other supervision, you may apply to the Board of Pardons and Parole for the restoration of some of those rights.

NOTICE TO UNDOCUMENTED NON-CITIZENS

In the event that you are not a citizen of the United States and are not in compliance with all the laws, rules and requirements concerning undocumented persons, upon conviction of any offense, you can expect to be taken into custody by the Department of Homeland Security for either prosecution or deportation.

PRELIMINARY HEARING

In the event your case is scheduled for a preliminary hearing, that hearing will be in the District Court before one of our four district court judges. The purpose of the preliminary hearing is for the State of Alabama to show or prove that there is probable cause that you committed the offense. Upon that finding of probable cause, the case will be bound over to the Grand Jury. If the Grand Jury makes a similar probable cause determination, an indictment will be returned and the case will be assigned to a Circuit Court Judge for trial before a jury.

It is in your interest to participate in the preliminary hearing because we will learn what the State's evidence will show. We can learn that by having a formal hearing or by waiving the case to the Grand Jury in which event the prosecutor will provide to us a copy of the police reports in the case. Cases are rarely won at Preliminary Hearing.

The decision of whether to have a formal hearing or whether to waive the case to the Grand Jury is yours. We normally benefit from waiving the case to the Grand Jury and receiving a copy of the prosecutor's file.

Trial Rights

As of this time, I will assume that you wish to take the case to trial and seek a jury verdict in your favor. The **decision** of whether to go to trial or to plead guilty **is yours** and yours alone. I will never tell you that you must plead guilty. However, if you become convinced during the course of the defense of this action that it is in your best interests to plead guilty, you must inform me and we will proceed accordingly.

We will now discuss your **trial rights** and **Appeal Rights** by reading them from the **Explanation of Rights and Plea of Guilty Form**. I am reading the form only for the purpose of informing you of those rights. I am certainly not trying to convince you to plead guilty.

In the event that <u>you</u> elect to plead guilty, you should do so only if you are actually guilty. As your attorney, I will never tell you to plead guilty. I will never direct you to do anything but to tell the truth. My job is to advise you of your rights at each step of the proceeding. **<u>YOU</u>** are the person who **must decide** what is in your best interest at each step of the proceeding. **I will advise you and I may recommend what I feel to be in your best interest, but <u>I will never tell you that you must plead guilty</u>!!**

In the event that you decide to plead guilty, we may enter into a **plea bargain** with the Assistant District Attorney prosecuting the case. In that event, you must realize that the **Plea Bargain** is a **RECOMMENDATION ONLY**. The Judge sentences you upon plea of guilty or jury verdict of guilty and must sentence you to a term within the range of punishment we just discussed. The Judge is **not** bound or obligated to follow the Plea Bargain and may reject the recommended plea bargain. If the judge refuses to accept the Plea Bargain, you will be given the opportunity to withdraw your guilty plea and go to trial.

IF YOU DECIDE TO GO TO TRIAL AND THERE IS A GUILTY VERDICT BY THE JURY, THE JUDGE HAS THE OPTION TO SENTENCE YOU UP TO THE MAXIMUM SENTENCE!!!! That is not to say that the judge will sentence you to the maximum, but the Judge has the authority to sentence you within the range of punishments to a sentence which is supported by the facts of the case and your history.

IF THERE IS A GUILTY PLEA, THE JUDGE IN ALL PROBABLILITY WILL SENTENCE ACCORDING TO THE PLEA BARGAIN WE WILL DISCUSS LATER.

WITNESSES

It will be necessary that **you** provide to me the names, addresses and phone numbers of any witnesses you wish to present at any hearing, trial or sentencing. The witnesses can be **character** witnesses or witnesses on the issue of guilt. It is also necessary that you provide to me any information which may relate to any defense, such as self-defense, insanity or alibi.

TRIAL PROCEDURE

It is in **CIRCUIT COURT** that we will have the **JURY TRIAL** of the case in the event you decide to plead **not guilty**. If you wish to **PLEA BARGAIN and plead guilty**, it is in Circuit Court that we will enter into plea negotiations with the **PROSECUTOR**.

In the event you decide to go to trial, we will have the right to participate in the **jury selection** process. You will have the right to be present during the selection of the jury and during the entire trial proceeding. The ultimate decision of whether you **testify** at your trial or not is yours. In the event you wish to testify, the State of Alabama will be able to present to the jury any prior **felony convictions and/or misdemeanor convictions involving dishonesty** that you may have. Any prior convictions would be offered to **impeach** your testimony or to reduce your credibility or believability. Additionally, the jury would then be aware of your past criminal history and likely would consider that in their deliberations.

In the event that you are tried and found guilty by the jury or if you plead guilty, the Circuit Judge will sentence you to imprisonment for a term within the range of punishments we have spoken of. We can **apply** for probation, work release or other programs which may be available. **The Judge has the discretion to grant or deny any application.** The Judge can impose a fine within the above range. The Judge will **ALWAYS** order payment of a Victim Compensation Assessment, court costs, the fee of the court appointed attorney, any mandatory fees and Restitution to the Victim, if any.

The Court, within its discretion, can sentence pursuant to the **Split Sentencing Act** to a combination of time to serve, work release or **PROBATION**.

In the event you are sentenced to a **split sentence**, you will be required to serve the split day for day and would not be eligible for release until the split is served.

In the event you should be sentenced to straight confinement in the **STATE PENITENTIARY** system, you will be **eligible** to be considered for **PAROLE** at the end of one-third (1/3) of the sentence imposed or ten (10) years, whichever is less. In the event you are convicted of any felony in this case, you will always be sentenced as an **HABITUAL OFFENDER** upon **later conviction** for any other felony. You may be eligible for any number of programs which can reduce the sentence you actually serve. Some inmates are eligible for good time reductions, work release, or others at the discretion of the Department of Corrections and the Board of Pardons and Parole. If you are sentenced in this case as an Habitual Offender, you may **NOT** be eligible for some programs.

If you are serving any other sentence at the time you plead guilty or are found guilty by a jury, the judge has the discretion to run any sentence you receive in this case either **concurrently with or consecutive to** the sentence you are now serving.

If you are sentenced to concurrent sentences on two different offenses, you will be given credit for time served awaiting trial in such a fashion as to require you to serve the longer of the two sentences.

If you are currently on probation for any offense, a conviction of the charge in this case will be considered by the Court to determine whether to revoke any suspended sentence in your previous case(s).

LESSER INCLUDED OFFENSES

For purposes of negotiation of a **Plea Bargain** or if there is a trial of his case, there may be consideration of **lesser included offenses**. Those are offenses which may be supported by the evidence which may be considered for settlement purposes or at the trial of the case. Lesser included offenses are offenses to which the charge may be reduced if supported by the evidence. If there is a reduction by negotiation or by jury verdict to a lesser included offense, the range of punishments will be reduced accordingly. We will talk about possible included offenses when the evidence is fully developed in your case.

CREDIT FOR TIME SERVED

Upon conviction by trial or by guilty pleas, at sentencing you will receive credit for all time spent in incarceration prior to the disposition of your case. However, pursuant to law and the policy of the Board of Pardons and Parole and Department of Corrections if you are convicted to two or more felonies and you are sentenced to concurrent sentences, you will receive credit for time served in the case in which you were incarcerated for the shortest period of time before disposition.

That is to say, if you are sentenced to concurrent sentences on two different offenses, you will be given credit for time served awaiting trial in such a fashion as to require you to serve the longer of the two sentences.

CORRECTIONAL INCENTIVE "GOOD" TIME

Inmates whose records in prison show that they have faithfully observed the disciplinary rules as prescribed are entitled to earn a deduction from their sentences as follows:

(1) 75 days for each 30 days actually served while the inmate classified as a Class I prisoner.

(2) 40 days for each 30 days actually served while the inmate classified as a Class II prisoner.

(3) 20 days for each 30 days actually served while the inmate classified as a Class III prisoner.

(4) No good time shall accrue while the inmate classified as a Class IV prisoner.

However, no person may receive the benefits of correctional incentive time if he or she has been convicted of a Class A felony or has been sentenced to life, or death, or who has received a sentence for more than 15 years. No person may receive the benefits of correctional incentive time if he or she has been convicted of a criminal sex offense of a child less than twelve years of age.

No inmate may be placed in Class I if he or she has been convicted of an assault where the victims of such assault suffered the permanent loss or use or permanent partial loss or use of any bodily organ or appendage. No person may be placed in Class I if he or she has been convicted of a crime involving the perpetration of sexual abuse upon the person of a child under the age of 17 years. Section 14-9-41(e), Code of Alabama of 1975.

SUPERVISED RE-ENTRY PROGRAM

If you should be sentenced to the state penitentiary to a term of confinement or to a split sentence, you may be eligible to be considered for the SRP program. Males are eligible when they are within one (1) year of your release (EOS) date. Females are eligible when they are within eighteen (18) months of their EOS date. Convictions for certain offenses will disqualify participation I the SRP program. Generally speaking, if you are convicted of a property crime, you will be eligible. If you are convicted of a sex offense, sale of drugs or an offense where a victim is physically harmed, you will generally not be eligible.

Appeal Rights

In the event you are convicted of any offense by **trial**, you have the right to appeal the conviction and sentence. To appeal, you must file a written notice of appeal with the Clerk of Circuit Court here in Madison County within Forty-Two (**42**) days of the date of sentencing. In the event you are indigent and cannot afford an attorney, a copy of the court's record or a copy of the transcript of any testimony, the Court can provide those to you at no cost to you.

We have covered the **limited right of appeal** of a **guilty plea** in the reading of the Explanation of Rights and Plea of Guilty form. You can appeal a guilty plea only in those two circumstances.

To win a case on appeal, we must be able to convince the Court of Criminal Appeals that the trial judge made a "**reversible error**." There is **no automatic**

reversal merely because you appeal. If you appeal the judge will set a **new bail on appeal** and you would have to post a **new bond** in order to be released during the appeal period. If the sentence is over 20 years, there will be no bail set on appeal and you would not be released from prison pending the appeal.

If you are successful on appeal, the case will be sent back to Circuit Court for a new trial. **The Court of Criminal Appeals does not reduce or modify sentences.**

ACKNOWLEDGEMENT

I, the undersigned defendant, acknowledge that my attorney, MITCHELL J. HOWIE, has read to me and discussed with me the information contained in the foregoing INFORMATION PAMPHLET and that I have been given notice of my Appeal Rights. I further **acknowledge the receipt of a copy** of the same, along with a copy of an Overview of the Pre-trial Intervention Program (PTIP) in Madison County (has been provided along with the offer of the PTIP Program if applicable to my case) and that a copy of the **indictment or warrant** and a copy of the Explanation of Rights and Plea of

Guilty Form will be provided upon request. I acknowledge that **I have the right to ask for further explanation at any time**. I acknowledge that **I understand the foregoing rights and information**.

________________________ __________________

DEFENDANT - CLIENT DATE

APPENDIX

Drug (Class A, B, C) Prison In/Out Worksheet

Eff. 10-1-2019

Defendant ____________________ Judge ____________________

Case No. ____________________ Prosecutor ____________________

Worksheet Preparer ____________________ Defense Attorney ____________________

Most Serious Conviction Offense — Please circle one *offense*

PRESUMPTIVE
***Class C** offenses*

Felony DUI	4
Poss of Marihuana 1st §13A-12-213(a)(1)	2
A/S/C Poss of Marihuana 1st §13A-12-213(a)(1)	2

PRESUMPTIVE
***Class B** offenses*

Manufacturing Controlled Substance 2nd	5
A/S/C Manufacturing Controlled Substance 2nd	5
Poss with Intent to Distribute Controlled Sub	5
A/S/C Poss with Intent to Distribute Controlled Sub	5
Sale/Distribution of Marihuana (other than to minor)	6
A/S/C Sale/Distribution of Marihuana (other than to minor)	6
Sale/Distribution of Schedule I-V (other than to minor)	6
A/S/C Sale/Distribution of Schedule I-V (other than to minor)	6

PRESUMPTIVE
***Class A** offenses*

Manufacturing Controlled Substance 1st	8
A/S/C Manufacturing Controlled Substance 1st	8

**A/S/C = Attempt/Solicitation/Conspiracy*

Score ☐

Number of Prior Adult Felony Convictions

None	0	3	5
1	2	4	6
2	3	5 or more	7

Score ☐

Number of Prior Adult Convictions for Misdemeanors or Violations

0-1	0	6-9	2
2-5	1	10 or more	3

Score ☐

Prior Incarceration with *Unsuspended* Sentence Imposed of 1 Year or More — 3 Score ☐

Prior Felony Probation or Parole Revocation — 1 Score ☐

Number of Prior Juvenile Delinquency or YO Adjudications (Violation/Misd/Felony)

None	0	3-4	2
1-2	1	5 or more	3

Score ☐

Possession/Use of a Deadly Weapon or Dangerous Instrument — 2 Score ☐

Total Score ☐

Disposition: ☑ **Presumptive**

1-7 points: Non-Prison **8 or more points: Prison**

Drug (Class A, B, C) Sentence Length Worksheet Eff. 10-1-2019

Defendant ______________________ Case No. ______________________

Most Serious Conviction Offense — Please circle one offense

PRESUMPTIVE
***Class C** offenses*

Felony DUI	76
Poss of Marihuana 1st §13A-12-213(a)(1)	71
A/S/C Poss of Marihuana 1st §13A-12-213(a)(1)	71

PRESUMPTIVE
***Class B** offenses*

Manufacturing Controlled Substance 2nd	105
A/S/C Manufacturing Controlled Substance 2nd	105
Poss with Intent to Distribute Controlled Sub	105
A/S/C Poss with Intent to Distribute Controlled Sub	105
Sale/Distribution of Marihuana (other than to minor)	84
A/S/C Sale/Distribution of Marihuana (other than to minor)	84
Sale/Distribution of Schedule I-V (other than to minor)	113
A/S/C Sale/Distribution of Schedule I-V (other than to minor)	113

PRESUMPTIVE
***Class A** offenses*

Manufacturing Controlled Substance 1st	286
A/S/C Manufacturing Controlled Substance 1st	286

**A/S/C = Attempt/Solicitation/Conspiracy*

Score [ ]

Number of Additional Felony Convictions (Including Counts)

None	0	3	44
1	15	4 or more	58
2	29		

Score [ ]

Number of Prior Adult Felony Convictions

None	0	3	30
1	10	4	40
2	20	5 or more	50

Score [ ]

Number of Prior Adult Felony Class C & Class D Convictions

None	0	4	28
1	7	5	35
2	14	6	43
3	21	7 or more	50

Score [ ]

Prior Incarceration with *Unsuspended* Sentence Imposed of 1 Year or More —— 14 **Score** [ ]

See Drug Sentence Length Table

☑ **Presumptive**

Total Score [ ]

Sentence Range _____ to _____ (straight) _____ to _____ (split)

Judge's Signature/Initial

____

Drug (Class D) Prison In/Out Worksheet

Eff. 10-1-2019

Defendant ____________________ Judge ____________________

Case No. ____________________ Prosecutor ____________________

Worksheet Preparer ____________________ Defense Attorney ____________________

Most Serious Conviction Offense — Please circle one *offense*

PRESUMPTIVE

***Class D** offenses*

Poss of Controlled Substance	1
A/S/C Poss of Controlled Substance	1
Poss of Marihuana 1st §13A-12-213(a)(2)	1
A/S/C Poss of Marihuana 1st §13A-12-213(a)(2)	1

**A/S/C = Attempt/Solicitation/Conspiracy*

Score ☐

Number of Prior Adult Felony Convictions

	None	0
	1	2
2 Class A or B felonies →	2	3
3 felonies →	3	5
	4	6
	5 or more	7

2 Class A or B felonies - If previously convicted of any two or more felonies that are Class A or Class B felonies and after such convictions has committed a Class D felony, upon conviction, he or she must be sentenced for a Class C felony but pursuant to the Drug (Class D) Prison Sentence Length Ranges for Worksheet (maximum of 120 months).

3 felonies - If previously convicted of any three or more felonies and after such convictions has committed a Class D felony, upon conviction, he or she must be sentenced for a Class C felony but pursuant to the Drug (Class D) Prison Sentence Length Ranges for Worksheet (maximum of 120 months).

Score ☐

Number of Prior Adult Convictions for Misdemeanors or Violations

0-1	0	6-9	2
2-5	1	10 or more	3

Score ☐

Prior Incarceration with *Unsuspended* Sentence Imposed of 1 Year or More — 3 **Score** ☐

Prior Felony Probation or Parole Revocation — 1 **Score** ☐

Number of Prior Juvenile Delinquency or YO Adjudications (Violation/Misd/Felony)

None	0	3-4	2
1-2	1	5 or more	3

Score ☐

Possession/Use of a Deadly Weapon or Dangerous Instrument — 2 **Score** ☐

Total Score ☐

Disposition: ☑ **Presumptive**

1-7 points: Non-Prison **8 or more points: Prison**

Drug (Class D) Sentence Length Worksheet

Eff. 10-1-2019

Defendant ____________________ Case No. ____________________

Most Serious Conviction Offense — Please circle one *offense*

PRESUMPTIVE
Class D offenses

Poss of Controlled Substance	59
A/S/C Poss of Controlled Substance	59
Poss of Marihuana 1st §13A-12-213(a)(2)	42
A/S/C Poss of Marihuana 1st §13A-12-213(a)(2)	42

**A/S/C = Attempt/Solicitation/Conspiracy*

Score [ ]

Number of Additional Felony Convictions (Including Counts)

None	0	3	44
1	15	4 or more	58
2	29		

Score [ ]

Number of Prior Adult Felony Convictions

	None	0
	1	10
2 Class A or B felonies →	2	20
3 felonies →	3	30
	4	40
	5 or more	50

2 Class A or B felonies - If previously convicted of any two or more felonies that are Class A or Class B felonies and after such convictions has committed a Class D felony, upon conviction, he or she must be sentenced for a Class C felony but pursuant to the Drug (Class D) Prison Sentence Length Ranges for Worksheet (maximum of 120 months)

3 felonies - If previously convicted of any three or more felonies and after such convictions has committed a Class D felony, upon conviction, he or she must be sentenced for a Class C felony but pursuant to the Drug (Class D) Prison Sentence Length Ranges for Worksheet (maximum of 120 months)

[ ]

Number of Prior Adult Felony Class C & Class D Convictions

None	0	4	28
1	7	5	35
2	14	6	43
3	21	7 or more	50

Score [ ]

Prior Incarceration with *Unsuspended* Sentence Imposed of 1 Year or More — 14 **Score** [ ]

See Drug Sentence Length Table

☑ **Presumptive**

Total Score [ ]

Sentence Range _____ to _____ (straight) _____ to _____ (split)

Judge's Signature/Initial

Drug (Class A, Class B) Prison Sentence Length Ranges for Worksheet

Time in Months

	Total Sentence			Time to Serve On Split		
Score	Low	Mid	High	Low	Mid	High
84	24	45	65	8	18	27
86	24	45	65	8	18	27
87	24	45	65	8	18	27
88	24	45	65	8	18	27
89	24	45	65	8	18	27
90	24	45	65	8	18	27
91	24	45	65	8	18	27
92	24	45	65	8	18	27
93	24	45	65	8	18	27
94	24	45	65	8	18	27
95	24	45	65	8	18	27
96	24	45	65	8	18	27
97	24	45	65	8	18	27
98	24	45	65	8	18	27
99	24	45	65	8	18	27
100	24	45	65	8	18	27
101	24	45	65	8	18	27
102	24	45	65	8	18	27
103	24	45	65	8	18	27
104	24	61	97	8	18	27
105	24	61	97	8	18	27
106	24	61	97	8	18	27
107	24	61	97	8	18	27
108	24	61	97	8	18	27
109	24	61	97	8	18	27
110	24	61	97	8	18	27
111	24	61	97	8	18	27
112	24	61	97	8	18	27
113	24	61	97	8	18	27
115	24	61	97	8	18	27
116	24	61	97	8	18	27
117	24	61	97	8	18	27
118	24	61	97	8	18	27
119	24	61	97	8	18	27
120	24	61	97	8	18	27
121	24	61	97	8	18	27
122	24	61	97	8	18	27
123	24	61	97	8	18	27
124	24	61	97	8	18	27
125	24	61	97	8	18	27
126	24	61	97	8	18	27
127	24	61	97	8	18	27
128	24	61	97	8	18	27
130	24	61	97	8	18	27
132	24	61	97	8	18	27
133	24	61	97	8	18	27
134	24	61	97	8	18	27
135	24	61	97	8	18	27
136	24	61	97	8	18	27
137	24	61	97	8	18	27
138	24	61	97	8	18	27
139	24	61	97	8	18	27

Drug (Class A, Class B) Prison Sentence Length Ranges for Worksheet

Time in Months

	Total Sentence			Time to Serve On Split		
Score	Low	Mid	High	Low	Mid	High
140	24	61	97	8	18	27
141	24	64	104	8	18	27
142	24	64	104	8	18	27
143	24	64	104	8	18	27
144	24	64	104	8	18	27
145	24	64	104	8	18	27
146	24	64	104	8	18	27
147	24	64	104	8	18	27
148	24	64	104	8	18	27
149	24	64	104	8	18	27
150	24	64	104	8	18	27
152	24	64	104	8	18	27
154	30	67	104	12	20	27
155	30	67	104	12	20	27
156	30	67	104	12	20	27
157	30	67	104	12	20	27
158	30	67	104	12	20	27
159	30	67	104	12	20	27
160	30	67	104	12	20	27
161	30	67	104	12	20	27
162	30	67	104	12	20	27
163	30	67	104	12	20	27
164	30	67	104	12	20	27
165	30	67	104	12	20	27
166	30	67	104	12	20	27
167	30	67	104	12	20	27
168	30	67	104	12	20	27
169	30	67	104	12	20	27
170	30	67	104	12	20	27
171	30	67	104	12	20	27
172	36	70	104	12	20	27
173	36	70	104	12	20	27
174	36	70	104	12	20	27
176	36	70	104	12	20	27
177	36	70	104	12	24	36
178	36	70	104	12	24	36
181	45	87	130	16	26	36
182	45	87	130	16	26	36
183	45	87	130	16	26	36
184	45	87	130	16	26	36
185	45	87	130	16	26	36
188	45	87	130	24	30	36
189	45	87	130	24	30	36
191	45	87	130	24	30	36
192	45	87	130	24	30	36
195	45	87	130	24	30	36
196	45	87	130	24	30	36
198	45	87	130	24	30	36
199	45	87	130	24	30	36
200	45	87	130	24	30	36
203	45	87	130	24	30	36
205	45	87	130	24	30	36

Drug (Class A, Class B) Prison Sentence Length Ranges for Worksheet

Time in Months

	Total Sentence			Time to Serve On Split		
Score	Low	Mid	High	Low	Mid	High
206	45	87	130	24	30	36
212	45	87	130	24	30	36
213	45	87	130	24	30	36
214	45	87	130	24	30	36
220	45	87	130	24	30	36
222	45	87	130	24	30	36
227	45	87	130	24	30	36
232	45	87	130	24	30	36
235	45	87	130	24	30	36
242	45	87	130	24	30	36
250	50	90	130	24	30	36
255	50	90	130	24	30	36
258	60	95	130	24	30	36
262	60	95	130	24	30	36
270	60	95	130	24	30	36
276	70	100	130	24	30	36
280	70	100	130	24	30	36
286	120	150	180	24	30	36
300	120	150	180	24	30	36
315	120	150	180	24	30	36
320	180	210	240	36	48	60
345	180	210	240	36	48	60
360	180	210	240	36	48	60
381	180	210	240	36	48	60

Drug (Class C) Prison Sentence Length Ranges for Worksheet

Time in Months

	Total Sentence			Time to Serve On Split		
Score	Low	Mid	High	Low	Mid	High
71	13	23	32	6	12	18
72	13	23	32	6	12	18
73	13	23	32	6	12	18
74	13	23	32	6	12	18
76	13	39	65	6	12	18
77	13	39	65	6	12	18
78	13	39	65	6	15	24
79	13	39	65	6	15	24
80	13	39	65	8	16	24
81	13	39	65	8	16	24
82	13	39	65	8	16	24
83	13	39	65	8	16	24
84	13	39	65	8	16	24
86	13	39	65	8	16	24
87	13	39	65	8	16	24
88	13	39	65	8	16	24
89	13	39	65	8	16	24
90	13	39	65	8	16	24
91	13	39	65	8	16	24
92	13	39	65	8	16	24
93	13	39	65	8	16	24
94	13	39	65	8	16	24
95	13	39	65	8	16	24
96	13	39	65	8	16	24
97	13	39	65	8	16	24
98	13	39	65	8	16	24
99	13	39	65	8	16	24
100	13	39	65	8	16	24
101	13	39	65	8	16	24
102	13	39	65	8	16	24
103	13	39	65	8	16	24
104	13	55	97	8	16	24
105	15	56	97	8	16	24
106	15	56	97	8	16	24
107	15	56	97	8	16	24
108	15	56	97	8	16	24
109	15	56	97	8	16	24
110	15	56	97	8	16	24
111	15	56	97	8	16	24
112	15	56	97	8	16	24
113	15	56	97	8	16	24
115	15	56	97	8	16	24
116	15	56	97	8	16	24
117	15	56	97	8	16	24
118	15	56	97	8	16	24
119	15	56	97	8	16	24
120	15	56	97	8	16	24
121	15	56	97	8	16	24
122	15	56	97	8	16	24
123	15	56	97	8	16	24
124	15	56	97	8	16	24
125	15	56	97	8	16	24
126	18	58	97	8	16	24
127	18	58	97	8	16	24
128	18	58	97	8	16	24

Drug (Class C) Prison Sentence Length Ranges for Worksheet

Time in Months

	Total Sentence			Time to Serve On Split		
Score	Low	Mid	High	Low	Mid	High
130	18	58	97	8	16	24
132	18	58	97	8	16	24
133	18	58	97	8	16	24
134	18	58	97	8	16	24
135	18	58	97	8	16	24
136	18	58	97	8	16	24
137	18	58	97	8	16	24
138	18	58	97	8	16	24
139	18	58	97	8	16	24
140	18	58	97	8	16	24
141	21	62	104	8	16	24
142	21	62	104	8	16	24
143	21	62	104	8	16	24
144	21	62	104	8	16	24
145	21	62	104	8	16	24
146	21	62	104	8	16	24
147	21	62	104	8	16	24
148	24	64	104	8	16	24
149	24	64	104	8	16	24
150	24	64	104	8	16	24
152	24	64	104	8	16	24
154	30	67	104	12	18	24
155	30	67	104	12	18	24
156	30	67	104	12	18	24
157	30	67	104	12	18	24
158	30	67	104	12	18	24
159	30	67	104	12	18	24
160	30	67	104	12	18	24
161	30	67	104	12	18	24
162	30	67	104	12	18	24
163	30	67	104	12	18	24
164	30	67	104	12	18	24
165	30	67	104	12	18	24
166	30	67	104	12	18	24
167	30	67	104	12	18	24
168	30	67	104	12	18	24
169	30	67	104	12	18	24
170	30	67	104	12	18	24
171	30	67	104	12	18	24
172	36	70	104	12	18	24
173	36	70	104	12	18	24
174	36	70	104	12	18	24
176	36	70	104	12	18	24
177	36	70	104	12	18	24
178	36	70	104	12	18	24
181	45	87	130	16	20	24
182	45	87	130	16	20	24
183	45	87	130	16	20	24
184	45	87	130	16	20	24
185	45	87	130	16	20	24
188	45	87	130	18	21	24
189	45	87	130	18	21	24
191	45	87	130	18	21	24
192	45	87	130	18	21	24
195	45	87	130	18	21	24

Drug (Class C) Prison Sentence Length Ranges for Worksheet

Time in Months

	Total Sentence			Time to Serve On Split		
Score	Low	Mid	High	Low	Mid	High
196	45	87	130	18	21	24
198	45	87	130	18	21	24
199	45	87	130	18	21	24
200	45	87	130	18	21	24
203	45	87	130	18	21	24
205	45	87	130	18	21	24
206	45	87	130	18	21	24
212	45	87	130	18	21	24
213	45	87	130	18	21	24
214	45	87	130	18	21	24
220	45	87	130	18	21	24
222	45	87	130	18	21	24
227	45	87	130	18	21	24
232	45	87	130	18	21	24
235	45	87	130	18	21	24
242	45	87	130	18	21	24
248	45	87	130	18	21	24

Drug (Class D) Prison Sentence Length Ranges for Worksheet

Time in Months

	Total Sentence			Time to Serve On Split		
Score	**Low**	**Mid**	**High**	**Low**	**Mid**	**High**
42	13	23	32	6	9	12
49	13	23	32	6	10	14
52	13	23	32	6	10	14
56	13	23	32	6	10	14
57	13	23	32	6	10	14
59	13	23	32	6	10	14
62	13	23	32	6	10	14
64	13	23	32	6	10	14
66	13	23	32	6	12	18
67	13	23	32	6	12	18
69	13	23	32	6	12	18
70	13	23	32	6	12	18
71	13	23	32	6	12	18
72	13	23	32	6	12	18
73	13	23	32	6	12	18
74	13	23	32	6	12	18
76	13	39	65	6	12	18
77	13	39	65	6	12	18
78	13	39	65	6	15	24
79	13	39	65	6	15	24
80	13	39	65	8	16	24
81	13	39	65	8	16	24
82	13	39	65	8	16	24
83	13	39	65	8	16	24
84	13	39	65	8	16	24
86	13	39	65	8	16	24
87	13	39	65	8	16	24
88	13	39	65	8	16	24
89	13	39	65	8	16	24
90	13	39	65	8	16	24
91	13	39	65	8	16	24
92	13	39	65	8	16	24
93	13	39	65	8	16	24
94	13	39	65	8	16	24
95	13	39	65	8	16	24
96	13	39	65	8	16	24
97	13	39	65	8	16	24
98	13	39	65	8	16	24
99	13	39	65	8	16	24
100	13	39	65	8	16	24
101	13	39	65	8	16	24
102	13	39	65	8	16	24
103	13	39	65	8	16	24
104	13	55	97	8	16	24
105	15	56	97	8	16	24
106	15	56	97	8	16	24
107	15	56	97	8	16	24
108	15	56	97	8	16	24
109	15	56	97	8	16	24
110	15	56	97	8	16	24
111	15	56	97	8	16	24
112	15	56	97	8	16	24
113	15	56	97	8	16	24
115	15	56	97	8	16	24
116	15	56	97	8	16	24
117	15	56	97	8	16	24

For Class D Felony Drug Sentence Length Scores greater than 75, a sentence greater than 60 months is only available if the defendant has been previously convicted of any three or more felonies or has been previously convicted of any two felonies that are Class A or Class B felonies.

Drug (Class D) Prison Sentence Length Ranges for Worksheet

Time in Months

	Total Sentence			Time to Serve On Split		
Score	Low	Mid	High	Low	Mid	High
118	15	56	97	8	16	24
119	15	56	97	8	16	24
120	15	56	97	8	16	24
121	15	56	97	8	16	24
122	15	56	97	8	16	24
123	15	56	97	8	16	24
124	15	56	97	8	16	24
125	15	56	97	8	16	24
126	18	58	97	8	16	24
127	18	58	97	8	16	24
128	18	58	97	8	16	24
130	18	58	97	8	16	24
132	18	58	97	8	16	24
133	18	58	97	8	16	24
134	18	58	97	8	16	24
135	18	58	97	8	16	24
136	18	58	97	8	16	24
137	18	58	97	8	16	24
138	18	58	97	8	16	24
139	18	58	97	8	16	24
140	18	58	97	8	16	24
141	21	62	104	8	16	24
142	21	62	104	8	16	24
143	21	62	104	8	16	24
144	21	62	104	8	16	24
145	21	62	104	8	16	24
146	21	62	104	8	16	24
147	21	62	104	8	16	24
148	24	64	104	8	16	24
149	24	64	104	8	16	24
150	24	64	104	8	16	24
152	24	64	104	8	16	24
154	30	67	104	12	18	24
155	30	67	104	12	18	24
156	30	67	104	12	18	24
157	30	67	104	12	18	24
158	30	67	104	12	18	24
159	30	67	104	12	18	24
160	30	67	104	12	18	24
161	30	67	104	12	18	24
162	30	67	104	12	18	24
163	30	67	104	12	18	24
164	30	67	104	12	18	24
165	30	67	104	12	18	24
166	30	67	104	12	18	24
167	30	67	104	12	18	24
168	30	67	104	12	18	24
169	30	67	104	12	18	24
170	30	67	104	12	18	24
171	30	67	104	12	18	24
172	36	70	104	12	18	24
173	36	70	104	12	18	24
174	36	70	104	12	18	24
176	36	70	104	12	18	24
177	36	70	104	12	18	24
178	36	70	104	12	18	24

For Class D Felony Drug Sentence Length Scores greater than 75, a sentence greater than 60 months is only available if the defendant has been previously convicted of any three or more felonies or has been previously convicted of any two felonies that are Class A or Class B felonies.

Drug (Class D) Prison Sentence Length Ranges for Worksheet

Time in Months

	Total Sentence			Time to Serve On Split		
Score	Low	Mid	High	Low	Mid	High
181	45	83	120	16	20	24
182	45	83	120	16	20	24
183	45	83	120	16	20	24
184	45	83	120	16	20	24
185	45	83	120	16	20	24
188	45	83	120	18	21	24
189	45	83	120	18	21	24
191	45	83	120	18	21	24
192	45	83	120	18	21	24
195	45	83	120	18	21	24
196	45	83	120	18	21	24
198	45	83	120	18	21	24
199	45	83	120	18	21	24
200	45	83	120	18	21	24
203	45	83	120	18	21	24
205	45	83	120	18	21	24
206	45	83	120	18	21	24
212	45	83	120	18	21	24
213	45	83	120	18	21	24
214	45	83	120	18	21	24
220	45	83	120	18	21	24
222	45	83	120	18	21	24
227	45	83	120	18	21	24

For Class D Felony Drug Sentence Length Scores greater than 75, a sentence greater than 60 months is only available if the defendant has been previously convicted of any three or more felonies or has been previously convicted of any two felonies that are Class A or Class B felonies.

Property (Class A, B, C) Prison In/Out Worksheet

Eff. 10-1-2019

Defendant ______________________ Judge ______________________

Case No. ______________________ Prosecutor ______________________

Worksheet Preparer ______________________ Defense Attorney ______________________

Most Serious Conviction Offense — Please circle one offense

PRESUMPTIVE *Class C offenses*		PRESUMPTIVE *Class B offenses*		VOLUNTARY	
Burglary 3rd §13A-7-7(a)(3)	11	Forgery 1st	10	Burglary 3rd (C) §13A-7-7(a)(1)&(2)	12
Forgery 2nd	9	Poss Forged Instrument 1st	10	Burglary 2nd (B)	13
Poss Forged Instrument 2nd	9	Receive Stolen Property 1st	10	Burglary 1st (A)	14
Receive Stolen Property 2nd	9	Theft of Lost Property 1st	10		
Theft of Lost Property 2nd	9	Theft of Property 1st	10		
Theft of Property 2nd	9	Theft of Services 1st	10		
Theft of Services 2nd	9				
Unauthorized Use/B&E Vehicle	9				

Score ☐

Number of Prior Adult Felony Convictions

None	0	3-4	2
1-2	1	5 or more	3

Score ☐

Number of Prior Adult Convictions for Same Felony

None	0	3-4	3
1	1	5 or more	4
2	2		

Score ☐

Number of Prior Adult Convictions for Misdemeanors or Violations

0-1	0	6-9	2
2-5	1	10 or more	3

Score ☐

Prior Incarceration with *Unsuspended* Sentence Imposed of 1 Year or More — 6 Score ☐

Prior Incarceration with *Unsuspended* Sentence Imposed of Less Than 1 Year — 3 Score ☐

Prior Felony Probation or Parole Revocation — 2 Score ☐

Number of Prior Juvenile Delinquency or YO Adjudications (Violation/Misd/Felony)

None	0	4	3
1	1	5 or more	4
2-3	2		

Score ☐

Possession/Use of a Deadly Weapon or Dangerous Instrument — 1 Score ☐

Injury to Victim — 2 Score ☐

Total Score ☐

Disposition: ☐ **Voluntary** ☐ **Presumptive**

8-14 points: Non-Prison **15 or more points: Prison**

Property (Class A, B, C) Sentence Length Worksheet Eff. 10-1-2019

Defendant ______________________ **Case No.** ______________________

Most Serious Conviction Offense Please circle one *offense*

PRESUMPTIVE *Class C offenses*		PRESUMPTIVE *Class B offenses*		VOLUNTARY	
Burglary 3rd §13A-7-7(a)(3)	47	Forgery 1st	58	Burglary 3rd (C) §13A-7-7(B)(1)&(2)	55
Forgery 2nd	47	Poss Forged Instrument 1st	58	Burglary 2nd (B)	70
Poss Forged Instrument 2nd	47	Receive Stolen Property 1st	58	Burglary 1st (A)	275
Receive Stolen Property 2nd	47	Theft of Lost Property 1st	58		
Theft of Lost Property 2nd	47	Theft of Property 1st	58		
Theft of Property 2nd	47	Theft of Services 1st	58		
Theft of Services 2nd	47				
Unauthorized Use/B&E Vehicle	47				

Score ☐

Number of Additional Felony Convictions (Including Counts)

None	0	2	10
1	5	3 or more	15

Score ☐

Number of Prior Adult Felony Convictions

None	0	6	72
1	12	7	84
2	24	8	97
3	36	9	109
4	48	10 or more	121
5	60		

Score ☐

Number of Prior Adult Felony Property Convictions

None	0	3	21
1	7	4	27
2	14	5 or more	34

Score ☐

Prior Incarceration with *Unsuspended* Sentence Imposed of 1 Year or More .... 15 **Score** ☐

Prior Felony Probation or Parole Revocation .... 7 **Score** ☐

Possession/Use of a Deadly Weapon/Dangerous Instrument or Injury to Victim .... 37 **Score** ☐

Acquired a Firearm During Offense .... 12 **Score** ☐

See Property Sentence Length Table **Total Score** ☐

☐ **Voluntary** ☐ **Presumptive**

Sentence Range _____ to _____ (straight) _____ to _____ (split)

Judge's Signature/Initial

____

Property (Class D) Prison In/Out Worksheet

Eff. 10-1-2019

Defendant ____________________ Judge ____________________

Case No. ____________________ Prosecutor ____________________

Worksheet Preparer ____________________ Defense Attorney ____________________

Most Serious Conviction Offense — Please circle one offense

PRESUMPTIVE *Class D offenses*		PRESUMPTIVE *Class D offenses*	
Forgery 3rd	8	Theft of Lost Property 3rd	8
Poss/Use Credit/Debit Card	8	Theft of Property 3rd	8
Poss Forged Instrument 3rd	8	Theft of Services 3rd	8
Receive Stolen Property 3rd	8		

Score ☐

Number of Prior Adult Felony Convictions

	None	0
	1	1
2 Class A or B felonies →	2	1
3 felonies →	3-4	2
	5 or more	3

2 Class A or B felonies - If previously convicted of any two or more felonies that are Class A or Class B felonies and after such convictions has committed a Class D felony, upon conviction, he or she must be sentenced for a Class C felony but pursuant to the Property (Class D) Prison Sentence Length Ranges for Worksheet (maximum of 120 months).

3 felonies - If previously convicted of any three or more felonies and after such convictions has committed a Class D felony, upon conviction, he or she must be sentenced for a Class C felony but pursuant to the Property (Class D) Prison Sentence Length Ranges for Worksheet (maximum of 120 months).

Score ☐

Number of Prior Adult Convictions for Same Felony

None	0	3-4	3
1	1	5 or more	4
2	2		

Score ☐

Number of Prior Adult Convictions for Misdemeanors or Violations

0-1	0	6-9	2
2-5	1	10 or more	3

Score ☐

Prior Incarceration with *Unsuspended* Sentence Imposed of 1 Year or More — 6 — Score ☐

Prior Incarceration with *Unsuspended* Sentence Imposed of Less Than 1 Year — 3 — Score ☐

Prior Felony Probation or Parole Revocation — 2 — Score ☐

Number of Prior Juvenile Delinquency or YO Adjudications (Violation/Misd/Felony)

None	0	4	3
1	1	5 or more	4
2-3	2		

Score ☐

Possession/Use of a Deadly Weapon or Dangerous Instrument — 1 — Score ☐

Injury to Victim — 2 — Score ☐

Total Score ☐

Disposition: ☑ **Presumptive**

8-14 points: Non-Prison **15 or more points: Prison**

Property (Class D) Sentence Length Worksheet

Eff.10-1-2019

Defendant ______________________ **Case No.** ______________________

Most Serious Conviction Offense — *Please circle one offense*

PRESUMPTIVE *Class D offenses*		PRESUMPTIVE *Class D offenses*	
Forgery 3rd	39	Theft of Lost Property 3rd	39
Poss/Use Credit/Debit Card	39	Theft of Property 3rd	39
Poss Forged Instrument 3rd	39	Theft of Services 3rd	39
Receive Stolen Property 3rd	39		

Score [ ]

Number of Additional Felony Convictions (Including Counts)

None	0	2	10
1	5	3 or more	15

Score [ ]

Number of Prior Adult Felony Convictions

	None	0
	1	12
2 Class A or B felonies →	2	24
	3	36
	4	48
	5	60
3 felonies →	6	72
	7	84
	8	97
	9	109
	10 or more	121

2 Class A or B felonies - If previously convicted of any two or more felonies that are Class A or Class B felonies and after such convictions has committed a Class D felony, upon conviction, he or she must be sentenced for a Class C felony but pursuant to the Property (Class D) Prison Sentence Length Ranges for Worksheet (maximum of 120 months).

3 felonies - If previously convicted of any three or more felonies and after such convictions has committed a Class D felony, upon conviction, he or she must be sentenced for a Class C felony but pursuant to the Property (Class D) Prison Sentence Length Ranges for Worksheet (maximum of 120 months).

Score [ ]

Number of Prior Adult Felony Property Convictions

None	0	3	21
1	7	4	27
2	14	5 or more	34

Score [ ]

Prior Incarceration with *Unsuspended* Sentence Imposed of 1 Year or More — 15 **Score** [ ]

Prior Felony Probation or Parole Revocation — 7 **Score** [ ]

Possession/Use of a Deadly Weapon/Dangerous Instrument or Injury to Victim — 37 **Score** [ ]

Acquired a Firearm During Offense — 12 **Score** [ ]

See Property Sentence Length Table **Total Score** [ ]

☑ **Presumptive**

Sentence Range _____ to _____ (straight) _____ to _____ (split)

Judge's Signature/Initial

____

Property (Class A, Class B) Prison Sentence Length Ranges for Worksheet

Time in Months

	Total Sentence			Time to Serve On Split		
Score	Low	Mid	High	Low	Mid	High
58	24	35	46	6	9	12
59	24	35	46	6	9	12
60	24	35	46	6	9	12
61	24	35	46	6	9	12
62	24	35	46	6	9	12
63	24	35	46	6	9	12
64	24	35	46	6	9	12
65	24	35	46	6	9	12
66	24	35	46	6	9	12
67	24	35	46	6	9	12
68	24	35	46	6	9	12
69	24	35	46	6	9	12
70	24	35	46	6	9	12
71	24	35	46	6	9	12
72	24	35	46	6	9	12
73	24	35	46	6	9	12
74	24	35	46	6	9	12
75	24	35	46	6	9	12
76	24	39	54	6	9	12
77	24	39	54	6	9	12
78	24	43	61	6	9	12
79	24	43	61	6	9	12
80	24	43	61	6	9	12
81	24	43	61	6	9	12
82	24	43	61	6	9	12
83	24	43	61	6	9	12
84	24	43	61	6	9	12
85	24	43	61	6	9	12
86	24	43	61	6	9	12
87	24	43	61	6	9	12
88	24	43	61	6	9	12
89	24	43	61	6	12	19
90	24	47	69	6	12	19
91	24	47	69	6	12	19
92	24	47	69	6	12	19
93	24	47	69	6	12	19
94	24	47	69	6	12	19
95	24	47	69	6	12	19
96	24	47	69	6	12	19
97	24	47	69	6	12	19
98	24	47	69	6	12	19
99	24	51	77	6	12	19
100	24	51	77	6	12	19
101	24	70	115	6	12	19
102	24	70	115	6	12	19
103	24	70	115	6	12	19
104	24	70	115	6	12	19
105	24	70	115	6	12	19
106	24	70	115	6	12	19
107	27	71	115	6	12	19
108	27	71	115	6	12	19
109	27	71	115	6	12	19

Property (Class A, Class B) Prison Sentence Length Ranges for Worksheet

Time in Months

	Total Sentence			Time to Serve On Split		
Score	Low	Mid	High	Low	Mid	High
110	27	71	115	6	12	19
111	27	71	115	6	12	19
112	27	71	115	6	12	19
113	27	71	115	6	12	19
114	27	71	115	6	12	19
115	27	71	115	6	12	19
116	27	71	115	6	12	19
117	27	71	115	6	12	19
118	32	74	115	6	12	19
119	54	85	115	6	12	19
120	54	85	115	6	12	19
121	54	85	115	6	12	19
122	54	85	115	6	12	19
123	54	85	115	6	12	19
124	54	85	115	6	12	19
125	54	85	115	6	12	19
126	54	85	115	6	12	19
127	54	85	115	6	12	19
128	54	85	115	6	12	19
129	54	85	115	6	12	19
130	54	85	115	6	12	19
131	54	85	115	6	12	19
132	54	85	115	6	12	19
133	54	85	115	6	12	19
134	54	85	115	6	12	19
135	54	85	115	6	12	19
136	54	85	115	6	12	19
137	54	85	115	6	12	19
138	54	85	115	6	12	19
139	54	85	115	6	12	19
140	54	85	115	6	12	19
141	54	85	115	6	12	19
142	54	85	115	6	12	19
143	54	85	115	6	12	19
144	76	95	115	6	12	19
145	76	95	115	6	12	19
146	76	95	115	6	12	19
147	76	95	115	6	12	19
148	76	95	115	6	12	19
149	76	95	115	6	12	19
150	76	95	115	6	12	19
151	76	95	115	12	15	19
152	76	95	115	12	15	19
153	76	95	115	12	15	19
154	76	95	115	12	15	19
155	76	95	115	12	15	19
156	76	95	115	12	15	19
157	76	95	115	12	15	19
158	76	95	115	12	15	19
159	76	95	115	12	15	19
160	76	95	115	12	15	19
161	76	95	115	12	15	19

Property (Class A, Class B) Prison Sentence Length Ranges for Worksheet

Time in Months

	Total Sentence			Time to Serve On Split		
Score	Low	Mid	High	Low	Mid	High
162	76	95	115	12	15	19
163	76	95	115	12	15	19
164	76	95	115	12	15	19
165	76	95	115	12	15	19
166	76	95	115	12	15	19
167	76	95	115	12	15	19
168	81	102	123	12	15	19
169	81	102	123	12	15	19
170	81	102	123	12	18	25
171	81	102	123	12	18	25
172	81	102	123	12	18	25
173	81	102	123	12	18	25
174	81	102	123	12	18	25
175	81	102	123	12	18	25
176	81	102	123	12	18	25
177	81	102	123	12	18	25
178	81	102	123	12	18	25
179	81	102	123	12	18	25
180	81	102	123	12	18	25
181	81	102	123	12	18	25
182	81	102	123	12	18	25
183	81	102	123	12	18	25
184	81	102	123	12	18	25
185	81	102	123	12	18	25
186	81	102	123	12	18	25
187	81	102	123	12	18	25
188	81	102	123	12	18	25
189	81	102	123	12	18	25
190	81	102	123	12	18	25
191	81	102	123	12	18	25
192	81	117	154	12	18	25
195	81	117	154	12	18	25
197	81	117	154	12	18	25
198	81	117	154	12	18	25
199	81	117	154	12	18	25
201	81	117	154	12	18	25
202	81	117	154	12	18	25
204	81	117	154	12	18	25
205	81	117	154	12	18	25
206	81	117	154	12	22	31
207	81	117	154	12	22	31
208	81	117	154	12	22	31
209	81	117	154	12	22	31
210	81	117	154	12	22	31
211	81	117	154	12	22	31
213	81	117	154	12	22	31
214	81	117	154	12	22	31
215	81	117	154	18	25	31
216	81	117	154	18	25	31
217	81	117	154	18	25	31
219	81	117	154	18	25	31
220	81	117	154	18	25	31

Property (Class A, Class B) Prison Sentence Length Ranges for Worksheet

Time in Months

	Total Sentence			Time to Serve On Split		
Score	Low	Mid	High	Low	Mid	High
222	81	117	154	18	25	31
223	81	117	154	18	25	31
225	81	117	154	18	25	31
228	81	117	154	18	25	31
232	81	117	154	18	25	31
233	81	117	154	18	25	31
235	81	117	154	18	25	31
245	81	117	154	18	25	31
246	81	117	154	18	25	31
250	81	117	154	18	25	31
260	81	117	154	18	25	31
274	81	117	154	18	25	31
275	120	135	156	24	30	36
280	120	135	156	24	30	36
282	120	135	156	24	30	36
285	120	135	156	24	30	36
287	120	135	156	24	30	36
290	120	135	156	24	30	36
292	120	135	156	24	30	36
294	120	135	156	24	30	36
299	120	135	156	24	30	36
302	120	135	156	24	30	36
304	120	135	156	24	30	36
306	120	135	156	24	30	36
308	120	135	156	24	30	36
309	120	135	156	24	30	36
311	120	135	156	24	30	36
312	120	135	156	24	30	36
313	120	135	156	24	30	36
314	120	135	156	24	30	36
317	120	135	156	24	30	36
318	120	150	180	24	30	36
320	120	150	180	24	30	36
321	120	150	180	24	30	36
323	120	150	180	24	30	36
324	120	150	180	24	30	36
326	120	150	180	24	30	36
329	120	150	180	24	30	36
331	120	150	180	24	30	36
333	120	150	180	24	30	36
335	120	150	180	24	30	36
336	120	150	180	24	30	36
338	120	150	180	24	30	36
339	120	150	180	24	30	36
341	120	150	180	24	30	36
342	120	150	180	24	30	36
343	120	150	180	24	30	36
345	120	150	180	24	30	36
347	120	150	180	24	30	36
350	120	150	180	24	30	36
351	120	150	180	24	30	36

Property (Class A, Class B) Prison Sentence Length Ranges for Worksheet

Time in Months

	Total Sentence			Time to Serve On Split		
Score	Low	Mid	High	Low	Mid	High
353	144	192	240	36	48	60
356	144	192	240	36	48	60
358	144	192	240	36	48	60
359	144	192	240	36	48	60
362	144	192	240	36	48	60
363	144	192	240	36	48	60
364	144	192	240	36	48	60
369	144	192	240	36	48	60
370	144	192	240	36	48	60
375	144	192	240	36	48	60
380	144	192	240	36	48	60
382	144	192	240	36	48	60
385	144	192	240	36	48	60
396	144	192	240	36	48	60
404	144	192	240	36	48	60
418	144	192	240	36	48	60

For Class A and Class B Felony Property Sentence Length Scores 353 to 418:
If a split sentence is selected for a score of 353 or higher, both the total sentence and the split portion must comport with the requirements of Ala. Code §15-18-8.

When the total sentence for a Class A or Class B felony is 15 years (180 months) or less, the maximum split portion is 3 years (36 months).

When the total sentence for a Class A or Class B felony is greater than 15 years (180 months) but does not exceed 20 years (240 months), the minimum split portion is 3 years (36 months) and the maximum split portion is 5 years (60 months).

Property (Class C) Prison Sentence Length Ranges for Worksheet

Time in Months

	Total Sentence			Time to Serve On Split		
Score	Low	Mid	High	Low	Mid	High
47	13	22	31	6	9	12
49	14	23	31	6	9	12
51	14	23	31	6	9	12
52	14	27	38	6	9	12
53	14	27	38	6	9	12
54	14	27	38	6	9	12
55	14	27	38	6	9	12
56	14	31	46	6	9	12
57	14	31	46	6	9	12
58	14	31	46	6	9	12
59	14	31	46	6	9	12
60	14	31	46	6	9	12
61	16	31	46	6	9	12
62	16	31	46	6	9	12
63	16	31	46	6	9	12
64	16	31	46	6	9	12
65	16	31	46	6	9	12
66	16	31	46	6	9	12
67	16	31	46	6	9	12
68	16	31	46	6	9	12
69	16	31	46	6	9	12
70	16	31	46	6	9	12
71	19	32	46	6	9	12
72	19	32	46	6	9	12
73	19	32	46	6	9	12
74	19	32	46	6	9	12
75	19	32	46	6	9	12
76	19	36	54	6	9	12
77	19	36	54	6	9	12
78	22	42	61	6	9	12
79	22	42	61	6	9	12
80	22	42	61	6	9	12
81	22	42	61	6	9	12
82	22	42	61	6	9	12
83	22	42	61	6	9	12
84	22	42	61	6	9	12
85	22	42	61	6	9	12
86	22	42	61	6	9	12
87	22	42	61	6	9	12
88	22	42	61	6	9	12
89	22	42	61	6	12	19
90	22	45	69	6	12	19
91	22	45	69	6	12	19
92	22	45	69	6	12	19
93	22	45	69	6	12	19
94	22	45	69	6	12	19
95	22	45	69	6	12	19
96	22	45	69	6	12	19
97	22	45	69	6	12	19
98	22	45	69	6	12	19
99	22	49	77	6	12	19
100	22	49	77	6	12	19

Property (Class C) Prison Sentence Length Ranges for Worksheet

Time in Months

	Total Sentence			Time to Serve On Split		
Score	Low	Mid	High	Low	Mid	High
101	22	68	115	6	12	19
102	22	68	115	6	12	19
103	22	68	115	6	12	19
104	22	68	115	6	12	19
105	22	68	115	6	12	19
106	24	70	115	6	12	19
107	27	71	115	6	12	19
108	27	71	115	6	12	19
109	27	71	115	6	12	19
110	27	71	115	6	12	19
111	27	71	115	6	12	19
112	27	71	115	6	12	19
113	27	71	115	6	12	19
114	27	71	115	6	12	19
115	27	71	115	6	12	19
116	27	71	115	6	12	19
117	27	71	115	6	12	19
118	32	74	115	6	12	19
119	54	85	115	6	12	19
120	54	85	115	6	12	19
121	54	85	115	6	12	19
122	54	85	115	6	12	19
123	54	85	115	6	12	19
124	54	85	115	6	12	19
125	54	85	115	6	12	19
126	54	85	115	6	12	19
127	54	85	115	6	12	19
128	54	85	115	6	12	19
129	54	85	115	6	12	19
130	54	85	115	6	12	19
131	54	85	115	6	12	19
132	54	85	115	6	12	19
133	54	85	115	6	12	19
134	54	85	115	6	12	19
135	54	85	115	6	12	19
136	54	85	115	6	12	19
137	54	85	115	6	12	19
138	54	85	115	6	12	19
139	54	85	115	6	12	19
140	54	85	115	6	12	19
141	54	85	115	6	12	19
142	54	85	115	6	12	19
143	54	85	115	6	12	19
144	76	95	115	6	12	19
145	76	95	115	6	12	19
146	76	95	115	6	12	19
147	76	95	115	6	12	19
148	76	95	115	6	12	19
149	76	95	115	6	12	19
150	76	95	115	6	12	19
151	76	95	115	12	15	19
152	76	95	115	12	15	19

Property (Class C) Prison Sentence Length Ranges for Worksheet

Time in Months

	Total Sentence			Time to Serve On Split		
Score	Low	Mid	High	Low	Mid	High
153	76	95	115	12	15	19
154	76	95	115	12	15	19
155	76	95	115	12	15	19
156	76	95	115	12	15	19
157	76	95	115	12	15	19
158	76	95	115	12	15	19
159	76	95	115	12	15	19
160	76	95	115	12	15	19
161	76	95	115	12	15	19
162	76	95	115	12	15	19
163	76	95	115	12	15	19
164	76	95	115	12	15	19
165	76	95	115	12	15	19
166	76	95	115	12	15	19
167	76	95	115	12	15	19
168	81	102	123	12	15	19
169	81	102	123	12	15	19
170	81	102	123	12	18	24
171	81	102	123	12	18	24
172	81	102	123	12	18	24
173	81	102	123	12	18	24
174	81	102	123	12	18	24
175	81	102	123	12	18	24
176	81	102	123	12	18	24
177	81	102	123	12	18	24
178	81	102	123	12	18	24
179	81	102	123	12	18	24
180	81	102	123	12	18	24
181	81	102	123	12	18	24
182	81	102	123	12	18	24
183	81	102	123	12	18	24
184	81	102	123	12	18	24
185	81	102	123	12	18	24
186	81	102	123	12	18	24
187	81	102	123	12	18	24
188	81	102	123	12	18	24
189	81	102	123	12	18	24
190	81	102	123	12	18	24
191	81	102	123	12	18	24
192	81	117	154	12	18	24
195	81	117	154	12	18	24
197	81	117	154	12	18	24
198	81	117	154	12	18	24
199	81	117	154	12	18	24
201	81	117	154	12	18	24
202	81	117	154	12	18	24
204	81	117	154	12	18	24
205	81	117	154	12	18	24
206	81	117	154	12	18	24
207	81	117	154	12	18	24
208	81	117	154	12	18	24
209	81	117	154	12	18	24

Property (Class C) Prison Sentence Length Ranges for Worksheet

Time in Months

Score	Total Sentence Low	Total Sentence Mid	Total Sentence High	Time to Serve On Split Low	Time to Serve On Split Mid	Time to Serve On Split High
210	81	117	154	12	18	24
211	81	117	154	12	18	24
213	81	117	154	12	18	24
214	81	117	154	12	18	24
215	81	117	154	18	21	24
216	81	117	154	18	21	24
217	81	117	154	18	21	24
219	81	117	154	18	21	24
220	81	117	154	18	21	24
222	81	117	154	18	21	24
223	81	117	154	18	21	24
225	81	117	154	18	21	24
228	81	117	154	18	21	24
232	81	117	154	18	21	24
233	81	117	154	18	21	24
235	81	117	154	18	21	24
245	81	117	154	18	21	24
246	81	117	154	18	21	24
250	81	117	154	18	21	24
260	81	117	154	18	21	24
274	81	117	154	18	21	24
275	81	119	156	18	21	24
280	81	119	156	18	21	24
282	81	119	156	18	21	24
285	81	119	156	18	21	24
287	81	119	156	18	21	24
288	81	119	156	18	21	24
296	81	119	156	18	21	24

Property (Class D) Prison Sentence Length Ranges for Worksheet

Time in Months

	Total Sentence			Time to Serve On Split		
Score	Low	Mid	High	Low	Mid	High
32	13	18	23	6	9	12
37	13	22	31	6	9	12
39	13	22	31	6	9	12
42	13	22	31	6	9	12
44	13	22	31	6	9	12
45	13	22	31	6	9	12
46	13	22	31	6	9	12
47	13	22	31	6	9	12
49	14	23	31	6	9	12
51	14	23	31	6	9	12
52	14	27	38	6	9	12
53	14	27	38	6	9	12
54	14	27	38	6	9	12
55	14	27	38	6	9	12
56	14	31	46	6	9	12
57	14	31	46	6	9	12
58	14	31	46	6	9	12
59	14	31	46	6	9	12
60	14	31	46	6	9	12
61	16	31	46	6	9	12
62	16	31	46	6	9	12
63	16	31	46	6	9	12
64	16	31	46	6	9	12
65	16	31	46	6	9	12
66	16	31	46	6	9	12
67	16	31	46	6	9	12
68	16	31	46	6	9	12
69	16	31	46	6	9	12
70	16	31	46	6	9	12
71	19	32	46	6	9	12
72	19	32	46	6	9	12
73	19	32	46	6	9	12
74	19	32	46	6	9	12
75	19	32	46	6	9	12
76	19	36	54	6	9	12
77	19	36	54	6	9	12
78	22	42	61	6	9	12
79	22	42	61	6	9	12
80	22	42	61	6	9	12
81	22	42	61	6	9	12
82	22	42	61	6	9	12
83	22	42	61	6	9	12
84	22	42	61	6	9	12
85	22	42	61	6	9	12
86	22	42	61	6	9	12
87	22	42	61	6	9	12
88	22	42	61	6	9	12
89	22	42	61	6	12	19
90	22	45	69	6	12	19
91	22	45	69	6	12	19
92	22	45	69	6	12	19
93	22	45	69	6	12	19
94	22	45	69	6	12	19

<u>For Class D Felony Property Sentence Length Scores 78 to 143</u>, a sentence greater than 60 months is only available if the defendant has been previously convicted of any three or more felonies or has been previously convicted of any two or more felonies that are Class A or Class B felonies.

Property (Class D) Prison Sentence Length Ranges for Worksheet

Time in Months

	Total Sentence			Time to Serve On Split		
Score	Low	Mid	High	Low	Mid	High
95	22	45	69	6	12	19
96	22	45	69	6	12	19
97	22	45	69	6	12	19
98	22	45	69	6	12	19
99	22	49	77	6	12	19
100	22	49	77	6	12	19
101	22	68	115	6	12	19
102	22	68	115	6	12	19
103	22	68	115	6	12	19
104	22	68	115	6	12	19
105	22	68	115	6	12	19
106	24	70	115	6	12	19
107	27	71	115	6	12	19
108	27	71	115	6	12	19
109	27	71	115	6	12	19
110	27	71	115	6	12	19
111	27	71	115	6	12	19
112	27	71	115	6	12	19
113	27	71	115	6	12	19
114	27	71	115	6	12	19
115	27	71	115	6	12	19
116	27	71	115	6	12	19
117	27	71	115	6	12	19
118	32	74	115	6	12	19
119	54	85	115	6	12	19
120	54	85	115	6	12	19
121	54	85	115	6	12	19
122	54	85	115	6	12	19
123	54	85	115	6	12	19
124	54	85	115	6	12	19
125	54	85	115	6	12	19
126	54	85	115	6	12	19
127	54	85	115	6	12	19
128	54	85	115	6	12	19
129	54	85	115	6	12	19
130	54	85	115	6	12	19
131	54	85	115	6	12	19
132	54	85	115	6	12	19
133	54	85	115	6	12	19
134	54	85	115	6	12	19
135	54	85	115	6	12	19
136	54	85	115	6	12	19
137	54	85	115	6	12	19
138	54	85	115	6	12	19
139	54	85	115	6	12	19
140	54	85	115	6	12	19
141	54	85	115	6	12	19
142	54	85	115	6	12	19
143	54	85	115	6	12	19
144	76	95	115	6	12	19
145	76	95	115	6	12	19
146	76	95	115	6	12	19
147	76	95	115	6	12	19

<u>For Class D Felony Property Sentence Length Scores 78 to 143</u>, a sentence greater than 60 months is only available if the defendant has been previously convicted of any three or more felonies or has been previously convicted of any two or more felonies that are Class A or Class B felonies.

Property (Class D) Prison Sentence Length Ranges for Worksheet

Time in Months

	Total Sentence			Time to Serve On Split		
Score	Low	Mid	High	Low	Mid	High
148	76	95	115	6	12	19
149	76	95	115	6	12	19
150	76	95	115	6	12	19
151	76	95	115	12	15	19
152	76	95	115	12	15	19
153	76	95	115	12	15	19
154	76	95	115	12	15	19
155	76	95	115	12	15	19
156	76	95	115	12	15	19
157	76	95	115	12	15	19
158	76	95	115	12	15	19
159	76	95	115	12	15	19
160	76	95	115	12	15	19
161	76	95	115	12	15	19
162	76	95	115	12	15	19
163	76	95	115	12	15	19
164	76	95	115	12	15	19
165	76	95	115	12	15	19
166	76	95	115	12	15	19
167	76	95	115	12	15	19
168	81	101	120	12	15	19
169	81	101	120	12	15	19
170	81	101	120	12	18	24
171	81	101	120	12	18	24
172	81	101	120	12	18	24
173	81	101	120	12	18	24
174	81	101	120	12	18	24
175	81	101	120	12	18	24
176	81	101	120	12	18	24
177	81	101	120	12	18	24
178	81	101	120	12	18	24
179	81	101	120	12	18	24
180	81	101	120	12	18	24
181	81	101	120	12	18	24
182	81	101	120	12	18	24
183	81	101	120	12	18	24
184	81	101	120	12	18	24
185	81	101	120	12	18	24
186	81	101	120	12	18	24
187	81	101	120	12	18	24
188	81	101	120	12	18	24
189	81	101	120	12	18	24
190	81	101	120	12	18	24
191	81	101	120	12	18	24
192	81	101	120	12	18	24
195	81	101	120	12	18	24
197	81	101	120	12	18	24
198	81	101	120	12	18	24
199	81	101	120	12	18	24
201	81	101	120	12	18	24
202	81	101	120	12	18	24
204	81	101	120	12	18	24
205	81	101	120	12	18	24

Property (Class D) Prison Sentence Length Ranges for Worksheet

Time in Months

	Total Sentence			Time to Serve On Split		
Score	Low	Mid	High	Low	Mid	High
206	81	101	120	12	18	24
207	81	101	120	12	18	24
208	81	101	120	12	18	24
209	81	101	120	12	18	24
210	81	101	120	12	18	24
211	81	101	120	12	18	24
213	81	101	120	12	18	24
214	81	101	120	12	18	24
215	81	101	120	18	21	24
216	81	101	120	18	21	24
217	81	101	120	18	21	24
219	81	101	120	18	21	24
220	81	101	120	18	21	24
222	81	101	120	18	21	24
223	81	101	120	18	21	24
225	81	101	120	18	21	24
228	81	101	120	18	21	24
232	81	101	120	18	21	24
233	81	101	120	18	21	24
235	81	101	120	18	21	24
245	81	101	120	18	21	24
246	81	101	120	18	21	24
250	81	101	120	18	21	24
260	81	101	120	18	21	24
274	81	101	120	18	21	24
275	81	101	120	18	21	24
280	81	101	120	18	21	24

Eff. 10-1-2019

Personal Prison In/Out Worksheet

Defendant ______________________ **Case No.** ______________________
Judge ______________________ **Prosecutor** ______________________
Probation Officer ______________________ **Defense Attorney** ______________________
Worksheet Preparer, Title ______________________ **Additional Cases** ______________________

Most Serious Conviction Offense — *Please circle one offense*

Assault 2nd	1	Rape 2nd, Sodomy 2nd, Robbery 2nd	5
Robbery 3rd	3	Rape 1st, Sodomy 1st, Manslaughter, Robbery 1st	8
Assault 1st	4	Murder	10

Score [ ]

Number of Prior Adult Felony Convictions

None	0
1	2
2	3
3	5
4	6
5 or more	8

Score [ ]

Prior Incarceration with *Unsuspended* Sentence Imposed of 1 Year or More

If Yes	1

Score [ ]

Number of Prior Juvenile Delinquency or YO Adjudications (Violation/Misd/Felony)

None	0
1-2	1
3-4	2
5 or more	3

Score [ ]

Possession/Use of Deadly Weapon or Dangerous Instrument

If Yes	4

Score [ ]

Recommendation

Total Score [ ]

1-7 points: Non-Prison **8 or more points: Prison**

Eff. 10-1-2019

Personal Prison Sentence Length Worksheet

Defendant ______________________________ Case No. ______________________

Most Serious Conviction Offense

Assault 2nd	72	Sodomy 1st	235
Sodomy 2nd	81	Manslaughter	238
Robbery 3rd	89	Robbery 1st	374
Rape 2nd	129	Rape 1st	386
Assault 1st	148	Murder	728
Robbery 2nd	173		

Score [ ]

Number of Prior Adult Felony Convictions

None	0
1	19
2	37
3	56
4	75
5	93
6	112
7	130
8	149
9	168
10 or more	186

Score [ ]

Number of Prior Incarcerations with *Unsuspended* Sentence Imposed of 1 Year or More

None	0
1	51
2	101
3	152
4	202
5 or more	253

Score [ ]

Prior Incarceration with *Unsuspended* Sentence Imposed of Less Than 1 Year

If Yes 33

Score [ ]

See Prison Sentence Length Recommendation Table

Total Score [ ]

Recommended Sentence Range _____ to _____ (straight) _____ to _____ (split)

Reason did **not** accept sentence length recommendation______________________________

____

Personal Sentence Length Ranges for Worksheet

Time in Months

	Total Sentence			Time to Serve On Split		
Score	Low	Mid	High	Low	Mid	High
72	13	37	60	6	15	24
81	13	37	60	6	15	24
89	13	37	60	6	15	24
91	13	37	60	6	15	24
100	13	37	60	6	15	24
105	13	47	80	6	15	24
108	13	47	80	6	15	24
109	13	47	80	6	15	24
122	13	47	80	6	15	24
123	13	47	80	6	15	24
124	13	47	80	6	15	24
126	13	47	80	6	15	24
128	13	47	80	6	15	24
129	39	71	102	6	15	24
132	47	74	102	12	18	24
133	47	74	102	12	18	24
137	47	74	102	12	18	24
141	55	78	102	12	18	24
142	55	99	143	12	24	36
145	55	99	143	12	24	36
147	55	99	143	12	24	36
148	55	99	143	12	24	36
156	55	99	143	12	24	36
159	62	103	143	12	24	36
160	62	103	143	12	24	36
162	62	103	143	12	24	36
164	62	103	143	12	24	36
166	62	108	153	12	24	36
167	78	116	153	12	24	36
169	78	116	153	12	24	36
170	78	116	153	12	24	36
173	78	116	153	12	24	36
175	78	116	153	12	24	36
177	78	116	153	12	24	36
178	78	116	153	12	24	36
179	78	116	153	12	24	36
180	78	116	153	12	24	36
181	78	116	153	12	24	36
182	78	116	153	12	24	36
184	78	116	153	12	24	36
185	78	116	153	12	24	36
192	78	126	173	12	24	36
193	78	126	173	12	24	36
196	78	126	173	12	24	36
197	78	126	173	12	24	36
198	78	126	173	12	24	36
199	78	126	173	12	24	36
200	78	126	173	12	24	36
201	78	126	173	12	24	36
204	78	126	173	12	24	36
206	78	126	173	12	24	36
209	78	126	173	12	24	36

Personal Sentence Length Ranges for Worksheet

Time in Months

	Total Sentence			Time to Serve On Split		
Score	Low	Mid	High	Low	Mid	High
210	78	126	173	12	24	36
215	78	126	173	12	24	36
217	78	126	173	12	24	36
218	78	126	173	12	24	36
219	78	126	173	12	24	36
223	78	126	173	12	24	36
224	78	126	173	12	24	36
225	78	126	173	12	24	36
227	78	126	173	12	24	36
229	78	126	173	12	24	36
230	78	126	173	12	24	36
231	78	126	173	12	24	36
232	78	126	173	18	29	40
233	78	126	173	18	29	40
235	78	126	173	18	29	40
236	78	126	173	18	33	48
237	78	126	173	18	33	48
238	78	126	173	18	33	48
243	78	126	173	18	33	48
248	78	141	204	18	33	48
249	78	141	204	18	33	48
251	78	141	204	18	33	48
252	78	141	204	18	33	48
253	78	141	204	18	33	48
254	86	145	204	18	33	48
255	86	145	204	18	33	48
256	86	145	204	18	33	48
257	86	145	204	18	33	48
260	86	145	204	18	33	48
261	86	145	204	18	33	48
262	86	145	204	18	33	48
265	86	145	204	18	33	48
266	86	145	204	18	33	48
267	86	145	204	18	33	48
268	86	145	204	18	33	48
269	86	145	204	18	33	48
271	86	145	204	18	33	48
272	86	145	204	18	33	48
274	86	145	204	18	33	48
275	86	145	204	18	33	48
276	86	145	204	18	33	48
280	86	145	204	18	33	48
281	86	145	204	18	33	48
283	101	153	204	18	33	48
286	101	153	204	18	33	48
287	101	153	204	18	33	48
288	101	153	204	18	33	48
289	101	153	204	18	33	48
290	101	153	204	18	33	48
291	101	153	204	18	33	48
292	101	153	204	18	33	48
294	101	153	204	18	33	48

Personal Sentence Length Ranges for Worksheet

Time in Months

	Total Sentence			Time to Serve On Split		
Score	Low	Mid	High	Low	Mid	High
299	101	153	204	18	33	48
300	101	153	204	18	33	48
305	101	153	204	18	33	48
307	101	153	204	18	33	48
308	101	153	204	18	33	48
311	101	153	204	22	41	60
313	101	153	204	22	41	60
316	101	153	204	22	41	60
317	101	153	204	22	41	60
319	101	153	204	22	41	60
322	101	153	204	22	41	60
323	101	153	204	22	41	60
324	101	153	204	22	41	60
326	117	161	204	22	41	60
330	117	161	204	22	41	60
331	117	161	204	22	41	60
332	117	161	204	22	41	60
334	117	161	204	22	41	60
335	117	161	204	22	41	60
336	117	161	204	22	41	60
337	117	161	204	22	41	60
338	117	161	204	22	41	60
339	117	161	204	24	42	60
342	117	161	204	24	42	60
344	117	161	204	24	42	60
345	117	161	204	24	42	60
349	117	161	204	24	42	60
350	117	161	204	24	42	60
355	117	161	204	24	42	60
356	117	161	204	24	42	60
358	117	161	204	24	42	60
359	117	161	204	24	42	60
362	117	161	204	24	42	60
363	117	161	204	24	42	60
364	117	161	204	24	42	60
366	117	161	204	24	42	60
367	117	161	204	24	42	60
371	117	186	255	24	42	60
373	117	186	255	24	42	60
374	117	186	255	24	42	60
375	117	186	255	24	42	60
376	117	186	255	24	42	60
378	117	186	255	24	42	60
379	117	186	255	24	42	60
381	117	186	255	24	42	60
386	117	186	255	24	42	60
387	117	186	255	24	42	60
389	117	186	255	24	42	60
393	117	186	255	24	42	60
400	117	186	255	24	42	60
403	117	186	255	24	42	60
404	117	186	255	24	42	60

Personal Sentence Length Ranges for Worksheet

Time in Months

	Total Sentence			Time to Serve On Split		
Score	Low	Mid	High	Low	Mid	High
405	117	186	255	24	42	60
406	117	186	255	24	42	60
407	117	186	255	24	42	60
409	117	186	255	24	42	60
411	117	186	255	24	42	60
412	117	186	255	24	42	60
414	117	186	255	24	42	60
418	117	186	255	24	42	60
419	117	186	255	24	42	60
423	117	186	255	24	42	60
425	117	186	255	24	42	60
426	117	186	255	24	42	60
427	117	186	255	24	42	60
428	117	186	255	24	42	60
430	117	186	255	24	42	60
431	117	186	255	24	42	60
436	117	186	255	24	42	60
437	117	186	255	24	42	60
438	156	231	306	24	42	60
439	156	231	306	24	42	60
442	156	231	306	24	42	60
444	156	231	306	24	42	60
449	156	231	306	24	42	60
450	156	231	306	24	42	60
451	156	231	306	36	48	60
455	156	231	306	36	48	60
456	156	231	306	36	48	60
457	156	231	306	36	48	60
458	156	231	306	36	48	60
460	156	231	306	36	48	60
461	156	282	408	36	48	60
462	156	282	408	36	48	60
463	156	282	408	36	48	60
465	156	282	408	36	48	60
467	156	282	408	36	48	60
470	156	282	408	36	48	60
474	156	282	408	36	48	60
475	156	282	408	36	48	60
476	156	282	408	36	48	60
477	156	282	408	36	48	60
483	156	282	408	36	48	60
487	156	282	408	36	48	60
491	156	282	408	36	48	60
493	156	282	408	36	48	60
494	156	282	408	36	48	60
495	156	282	408	36	48	60
498	156	282	408	36	48	60
500	156	282	408	36	48	60
501	156	282	408	36	48	60
505	156	282	408	36	48	60
506	156	588	1020	36	48	60
507	156	588	1020	36	48	60

Personal Sentence Length Ranges for Worksheet

Time in Months

	Total Sentence			Time to Serve On Split		
Score	Low	Mid	High	Low	Mid	High
510	156	588	1020	36	48	60
512	156	588	1020	36	48	60
513	156	588	1020	36	48	60
520	156	588	1020	36	48	60
524	156	588	1020	36	48	60
526	156	588	1020	36	48	60
528	156	588	1020	36	48	60
529	156	588	1020	36	48	60
530	156	588	1020	36	48	60
531	156	588	1020	36	48	60
533	156	588	1020	36	48	60
540	156	588	1020			
543	156	588	1020			
544	156	588	1020			
545	156	588	1020			
548	156	588	1020			
550	156	588	1020			
551	156	588	1020			
552	156	588	1020			
553	156	588	1020			
556	156	588	1020			
558	156	588	1020			
562	156	588	1020			
564	156	588	1020			
582	156	588	1020			
590	156	588	1020			
594	156	588	1020			
595	156	588	1020			
601	156	588	1020			
602	156	588	1020			
607	156	588	1020			
619	156	588	1020			
620	156	588	1020			
627	156	588	1020			
632	156	588	1020			
652	156	588	1020			
665	156	588	1020			
676	156	588	1020			
677	156	588	1020			
684	156	588	1020			
688	156	588	1020			
695	156	588	1020			
701	156	588	1020			
706	156	588	1020			
709	156	588	1020			
710	156	588	1020			
728	156	588	1020			
732	156	588	1020			
735	234	627	1020			
747	234	627	1020			
757	234	627	1020			
761	234	627	1020			

Personal Sentence Length Ranges for Worksheet

Time in Months

	Total Sentence			Time to Serve On Split		
Score	Low	Mid	High	Low	Mid	High
765	234	627	1020			
780	234	627	1020			
784	234	627	1020			
790	234	627	1020			
798	234	627	1020			
803	234	627	1020			
812	234	627	1020			
816	234	627	1020			
817	234	627	1020			
831	234	627	1020			
835	234	627	1020			
836	234	627	1020			
840	234	627	1020			
848	234	627	1020			
849	234	627	1020			
854	234	627	1020			
868	234	627	1020			
872	234	627	1020			
885	234	627	1020			
904	234	627	1020			
905	234	627	1020			
918	234	627	1020			
936	234	627	1020			
950	234	627	1020			
955	234	627	1020			
986	234	627	1020			
1010	234	627	1020			
1111	234	627	1020			
1126	234	627	1020			
1130	234	627	1020			

WHAT IS THE NEXT STEP?

Whether you are charged with simple possession of drugs or a violent crime, the Huntsville criminal defense lawyers at the Law Office of Mitchell J. Howie & Associates, P.L.L.C. can help you when you need it most! If you are not located in Alabama, please use this guide to secure representation in the jurisdiction you are located in.

Criminal Defense Attorneys at the Law Office of Mitchell J. Howie & Associates, P.L.L.C. will zealously and aggressively represent your interests in the criminal justice system when you need the help the most.

Visit us at www.mitchellhowie.com or call us today at 256-533-8074 for an initial consultation.

INDEX

Notes

Made in the USA
Monee, IL
03 November 2026

67387926R00085